Praise for Y

'In *You Lead*, Minter Dial has written a refreshingly original necessary book on leadership. By helping leaders be themselves – and better versions of themselves, at that – this form of new leadership will help drive not just better engagement, performance and business results; it will also help towards improving another important issue, which is mental health and wellbeing in the workplace. A must-read.' SUKI THOMPSON, FOUNDER AND CEO, LET'S RESET, EXECUTIVE DIRECTOR, XEIM AND CHAIR, OYSTERCATCHERS

'*You Lead* is a STOP PRESS MUST-READ. As Minter Dial points out, the great leaders of tomorrow will be those who know how to be themselves consistently throughout the day, whether it's with the cashier at the local grocer or one's spouse, friend, client, distributor or colleague. This book draws out a practical way to be such a leader, all the while keenly delivering on results. *You Lead* is a complete leadership guide.' NICOLAS BORDAS, VICE-PRESIDENT INTERNATIONAL, TBWA/WORLDWIDE AND BOARD MEMBER, OMNICOM EUROPE

'A great read, a real guide for evolving your leadership skills and style using proven strategies while incorporating the new realities of today's rapidly changing business environment. It is especially helpful in understanding the impact of the digital revolution and how to master those skills as part of the *You Lead* philosophy. I highly recommend this to leaders both seasoned and those developing leaders of tomorrow!' PAT PARENTY, FORMER PRESIDENT, L'ORÉAL PROFESSIONAL PRODUCTS DIVISION USA

'I met Minter Dial over a decade ago, during his time at L'Oréal. Over the years, I have met thousands of executives. I've only maintained a friendship with a small few. Minter is one of the few. This book explains why. He is a leader – through and through. Mostly, because he leads himself with excellence. He has humility, courage, a deep sense of empathy for himself, his team members and the customer. Most importantly, he is curious. These are just some of the ingredients that make him great. Those are just some of the ingredients in his excellent new book, *You Lead*, that will make you great. Times are crazy. They are going to get crazier. You lead!' MITCH JOEL, AUTHOR OF *SIX PIXELS OF SEPARATION* AND *CTRL ALT DELETE*

'Minter Dial brings his considerable professional experience and personal skills to delineate the core principles of management. Excellent counsel as to how to move from intention to execution. A worthy read.' ALAN TREFLER, FOUNDER AND CEO, PEGASYSTEMS

'Shakespeare said: "To be or not to be, that is the question". Gordon Sumner (Sting) answered him a few centuries later: "Be yourself, no matter what they say". Minter Dial is an overarching combination between Shakespeare and Sting, a writer and a musician. And you should read that book for sure, *and* listen to that book, one of the most practical and musical I have had in my hands for a decade.' LAURENT CHOAIN, CHIEF OF PEOPLE, EDUCATION AND CULTURE, MAZARS GROUP

'What am I doing that matters? The answer lies within according to Minter Dial in this inspirational book.' MARK SCHAEFER, AUTHOR OF *MARKETING REBELLION*

'A thoughtful, honest and well-researched reminder of how important it is to be yourself in business. Both customers and employees gravitate towards those who feel genuine passion about their brand, because it really does show. As Minter Dial says, it is in every business leader's interests to focus on making the world around you a better place, rather than simply thinking about making yourself better off. I couldn't have put it better myself.' ANNE BODEN, FOUNDER AND CEO, STARLING BANK

'If Peter Thiel wrote *Zero to One* for entrepreneurs, Minter Dial has written the *Zero to One* for leaders. In *You Lead*, he makes a most compelling case for why we should bring our entire selves to work, lead from within and do things that matter.' SOPHIE DEVONSHIRE, AUTHOR OF *SUPERFAST* AND CEO, THE MARKETING SOCIETY

'When we radiate our passions to the world, the relationship we build with our customers becomes more important than the products and services we sell them. You will find these and other often surprising ideas in this little book of big ideas where Minter Dial shares the essence of how to lead both small and large organizations.' DAVID MEERMAN SCOTT, *WALL STREET JOURNAL* BESTSELLING AUTHOR OF *FANOCRACY*

'"Lead" is a better verb than it is a noun. Minter Dial's book gives you an actionable blueprint for a new way of looking at leading, starting with yourself.' ANN HANDLEY, *WALL STREET JOURNAL* BESTSELLING AUTHOR AND CHIEF CONTENT OFFICER, MARKETINGPROFS

'In *You Lead*, Minter Dial adroitly pulls together how you can bring your full self to work and deliver on results.' CHARLENE LI, *NEW YORK TIMES* BESTSELLING AUTHOR OF *THE DISRUPTION MINDSET* AND SENIOR ANALYST, ALTIMETER

'The specific, intertwined skills, behaviours and talents to become a more successful leader are described as actionable insights in this idea-packed book to support us in our work. They include apt use of technology, messaging, speed learning, customer-centricity and considerably more. Clearly the author has first-hand knowledge of what he advocates, making it a credible, valuable read.' KARE ANDERSON, TED SPEAKER AND AUTHOR

'It's about time this book was written. In *You Lead*, Minter Dial vividly captures a dynamic change in today's society – that our business, government, and educational leaders need to stand up for doing what is right before it becomes an issue. That to be a successful leader in today's world it requires courageously bringing our whole selves to the table: professionally and personally. The result is a passionate call to arms, urging all of us to get in touch with who we are so that we can lead in a way that is true to our life experiences, ethics and values. This new book is undoubtedly one of the most important books written for our times. You'll need two copies!' CHARLENE LAIDLEY, FOUNDER, FUTUREPROOF: CREATING A GENDER EQUAL WORLDTM, UN WOMEN GLOBAL CHAMPION FOR CHANGE, AND LONDON TECH WEEK 30 CHANGE MAKER'S TO WATCH

'Minter Dial has a way of getting right to the heart of the biggest issues a business leader faces today. He writes in a way that is thought-provoking and challenging. Be warned – when you read *You Lead* you are going to feel uncomfortable about changes you should have made already. But you'll also be inspired to rethink and adjust your approach. It's one of the few leadership books I've read that refers to the customer as much as the team and the leader themselves.' DIANE YOUNG, CO-FOUNDER AND CEO, THE DRUM

'When someone asks you to read another leadership book mine tends to be an allergic reaction expecting another lecture on who you should be and little recognition of who you are. So when I saw the fly sheet of *You Lead* and read "How being yourself makes you a better leader" I was not just pleasantly surprised but intrigued. *You Lead* is a compelling read for those like me who believe leadership is personal and authenticity is the gateway to discovering the leader in each of us. Read it and you might just learn about yourself on your journey to leadership.' RONAN DUNNE, CEO, VERIZON CONSUMER GROUP

'*You Lead* delivers actionable concepts and useful examples of the leadership skills you need to advance in the coming years. Study this valuable book and apply these formulas to supercharge your own leadership practice. Well worth your time!' CHRIS BROGAN, *NEW YORK TIMES* AND *WALL STREET JOURNAL* BESTSELLING AUTHOR AND FOUNDER, STORYLEADER™

You Lead

*How being yourself makes you
a better leader*

Minter Dial

KoganPage

Publisher's note
Every possible effort has been made to ensure that the information contained in this book is accurate at the time of going to press, and the publishers and author cannot accept responsibility for any errors or omissions, however caused. No responsibility for loss or damage occasioned to any person acting, or refraining from action, as a result of the material in this publication can be accepted by the editor, the publisher or the author.

First published in Great Britain and the United States in 2021 by Kogan Page Limited

Apart from any fair dealing for the purposes of research or private study, or criticism or review, as permitted under the Copyright, Designs and Patents Act 1988, this publication may only be reproduced, stored or transmitted, in any form or by any means, with the prior permission in writing of the publishers, or in the case of reprographic reproduction in accordance with the terms and licences issued by the CLA. Enquiries concerning reproduction outside these terms should be sent to the publishers at the undermentioned addresses:

2nd Floor, 45 Gee Street
London
EC1V 3RS
United Kingdom
www.koganpage.com

122 W 27th St, 10th Floor
New York, NY 10001
USA

4737/23 Ansari Road
Daryaganj
New Delhi 110002
India

Kogan Page books are printed on paper from sustainable forests.

© Minter Dial, 2021

The right of Minter Dial to be identified as the author of this work has been asserted by him in accordance with the Copyright, Designs and Patents Act 1988.

ISBNs
Hardback   978 1 78966 627 4
Paperback   978 1 78966 625 0
Ebook   978 1 78966 626 7

British Library Cataloguing-in-Publication Data

A CIP record for this book is available from the British Library.

Library of Congress Cataloging-in-Publication Data

Names: Dial, Minter, 1964- author.
Title: You lead : how being yourself makes you a better leader / Minter Dial.
Description: 1 Edition. | New York : Kogan Page Inc, 2021. | Includes
    bibliographical references and index.
Identifiers: LCCN 2020043302 (print) | LCCN 2020043303 (ebook) | ISBN
    9781789666250 (paperback) | ISBN 9781789666274 (hardback) | ISBN
    9781789666267 (ebook)
Subjects: LCSH: Leadership–Psychological aspects. | Personality. | Social interaction.
Classification: LCC HM1261 .D523 2021 (print) | LCC HM1261 (ebook) | DDC
    158/.4–dc23
LC record available at https://lccn.loc.gov/2020043302
LC ebook record available at https://lccn.loc.gov/2020043303

Typeset by Hong Kong FIVE Workshop
Print production managed by Jellyfish
Printed and bound by CPI Group (UK) Ltd, Croydon CR0 4YY

CONTENTS

List of Figures xii
Foreword xiii
Preface xv
Gratefulness and acknowledgements xvii

PART ONE
Setting the stage: The wake-up call for a new form of
leadership 1

1 It's a rocky world 6
  Making values come alive 6
  Branding is personal 15
  Scaling the digital mountain 19
  Recap of key messages and actionable points 26
  Endnotes 27

2 Got the right governance, Guv'nor? 28
  Staying critical 29
  Assessing ownership structure 30
  How to establish an ethical construct 46
  Governing data and data transformation 49
  Recap of key messages and actionable points 50
  Endnotes 51

3 Life is work, too 54
  The AND mindset 55
  Charting your North Star setting 56
  Business cases: LEGO and L'Oréal 64
  Paradox 1: We need to belong, yet be different 66
  Paradox 2: We need to understand our past, yet live for the
    future 71

Paradox 3: We must reconcile the quest for order in the presence of chaos 78
Paradox 4: We seek truth but gravitate towards stories 80
Recap of key messages and actionable points 83
Endnotes 84

PART TWO
Merging the personal with the professional 87

4 CHECK: Your model of leadership 91
Check your mindset 94
Curiosity 95
Humility 97
Empathy 102
Courage 106
Karmic 110
Recap of key messages and actionable points 115
Endnotes 116

5 Employee-first customer-centricity 118
Leading from within 119
The Inside-Out model 120
The partner mindset 123
What do you stand for? 125
Loyalty to the core 127
Creating a meaningful community 131
Crafting uniqueness 138
How to make purpose come alive – imperfectly 141
Recap of key messages and actionable points 142
Endnotes 143

6 Making customer-centricity come alive 145
Relating customer-centricity to the customer experience 147
The customer-centric mindset 150
Measuring customer-centricity 155

The role of data in the customer experience 158
Putting the customer into service 162
What does real customer-centricity look like? 163
Recap of key messages and actionable points 168
Endnotes 169

PART THREE
The challenges and realities of implementation: The personal
journey 171

7 The art of being a leader 177
Being: the power of being versus doing 177
Time: because it's your rarest resource 182
People: leading from within 186
Recap of key messages and actionable points 194
Endnotes 194

8 Leadership in practice 196
Communicating: because communications are the lifeblood
   of the organization 196
Learning: because it's an ever-changing world 205
Recap of key messages and actionable points 210
Endnotes 211

9 Connecting the dots 212
Strategic transformation: changing minds and culture 213
Believe in the process: let go of some old tenets 214
The Connector-in-Chief: at your service 216
Building your network: it takes work 217
Imperfection: embrace your foibles 218
Fair and firm: understand and be understood 220
Business as a force for good: inside and out 221
Endnote 223

Index 224

LIST OF FIGURES

Figure 1.1   Embracing the divide between professional and personal spheres **19**

Figure 1.2   Scaling the digital mountain **21**

Figure 2.1   Triple axis ownership and governance **31**

Figure 2.2   Corporate versus commercial brand names **35**

Figure 2.3   Apple versus Samsung Electronics stock price performance: June 2015 to June 2020 **37**

Figure 2.4   Publicly traded or privately held **40**

Figure 2.5   Founder family presence **44**

Figure 3.1   Defining your direction in three steps **58**

Figure 3.2   Aligning personal and professional **59**

Figure 3.3   Agency: individuals seeking their tribe/ community **68**

Figure 3.4   If individuals don't feel recognized, they flee **69**

Figure 5.1   Leading from within and the Inside-Out model **120**

Figure 5.2   Redken Inside-Out model **122**

Figure 5.3   Partner mindset **124**

Figure 5.4   The Brand Tattoo test **135**

Figure 5.5   Branding along the chain of value **139**

Figure 5.6   Employee-first communications **140**

Figure 6.1   The human factor in the customer journey **147**

Figure 6.2   Orientations that encumber customer-centricity **152**

Figure 6.3   Virtuous or vicious cycle **160**

FOREWORD

Whether you're leading at the top of a conglomerate, a start-up or a small team within a larger organization, there's no doubt that leadership needs to do a major step change to adapt to the new world order of constant commotion. I've had the good fortune to work with some of the very top leaders in the world, including Sir Richard Branson, Steve Jobs and Charles Schwab, as well as the founders of some of the most exciting and enterprising start-ups, including LYFT CEO and co-founder Logan Green and Pinterest co-founder Evan Sharp. What I've observed from these standout leaders is that great leadership is a journey. No one is born a leader. It is a quality you craft, hone and earn over time. More than ever before, to be a great leader is a journey where the personal and professional ambitions and qualities must find a harmony, if not merge together. As I wrote about in my last book, *Admired*, there's a very personal nature to gaining respect and admiration for your Most Valuable People (MVP) in your life and work.

In his latest book, *You Lead*, Minter Dial draws out a cogent path for leaders like yourself to evolve by allowing if not exhorting you to lean in on your personal values, develop a greater self-awareness and make sure that what you do matters, for you and those around you, including your circle of MVPs. It's a personal journey that Minter leads you on, filled with stories and missteps from which to learn. Like myself, Minter loves music and leads by example in talking about how his personal passions contributed to developing his personality, impacting his sense of self and informing his leadership style. As I like to say, you can only grow and scale your business as fast as you grow and scale yourself.

If technology has been generally credited with driving the pace of change, we have all experienced in the last year how the forces of disruption can also be different in nature and scope. Whether leading through the pandemic, through the Black Lives Matter social movement or through challenging economic times, we can best adjust the rudder of our ship when we are in touch with ourselves and have an honest relationship with those around us, to do things that matter. As such the ship in leadership will steer a brighter course through the turbulence.

I've known Minter since his days as a senior executive at L'Oréal. He is someone who has always bravely walked the talk. This book is a shining example.

Mark C Thompson

Mark C Thompson is the World's No. 1 Leadership Coach for Transformational Growth, Team Engagement and Driving Change, according to the American Management Association. He is also the author of the *New York Times* bestselling books *Admired: 21 ways to double your value*, *Now Build a Great Business* and *Success Built to Last: Creating a life that matters*.

PREFACE

If writing a book is a labour of love, it seems more and more that reading one is a love of labour. Yet, I want to acknowledge and thank you as you've chosen to read *You Lead*. Where writing for this book started in the autumn of 2019 and continued through the entire first half of 2020, you are reading this at a later time, after the US presidential elections and certainly many other new events that have impacted the world around us. If during the period of writing this book, the context changed in dramatic fashion, it's bound to continue shifting and evolving. In the process of writing through the pandemic and the Black Lives Matter movement, I feel ever more convinced that the content of this book has become even more relevant. We need a new form of leadership up and down society, in government and, most definitely, in business. Whether we're leading within big business, running a start-up or working in a non-governmental organization, we can and should take a hard look at ourselves and our environment, and lean in on what matters. Being yourself takes knowing yourself. By being more in touch with who you are, you'll not only be a better leader, you'll also be a better person. Business can be a force for change for good, all the while competing and performing at the highest level.

Taking a page out of the physics playbook, as the compelling energy and climate expert Jean-Marc Jancovici says, we know that transformation requires energy.[1] In the context of leadership, with the ever-increasing constraints (economic, environmental, social or sanitary), we will need to generate an extra level of energy within ourselves and our organization in order to adapt and transform. The only way to succeed long term is to offer a sense of purpose that taps into our discretionary energy.

It's up to us as leaders to set the example.

As you go through the book, you will find key insights and messages along with actionable points at the end of each chapter. If you go to www.minterdial.com/you-lead (archived at https://perma.cc/L6CC-9XFM), you will find further resources, including some exercises, recommended books, podcasts and articles, as well as the detailed results of an exclusive leadership survey that is featured in Chapters 3 and 4. There'll also be a space to start or join a conversation as provoked by what you've read.

Endnote

1. jancovici.com/en/energy-transition/energy-and-us/what-is-energy-actually/ (archived at https://perma.cc/2M8C-MNKR)

GRATEFULNESS AND ACKNOWLEDGEMENTS

No man is an island and no published author is truly alone. I want to thank my editor, Géraldine Collard, for her patience, kind encouragement and refined direction throughout the writing, including pulling it all together right after the pandemic lockdown was eased and through the persistent concussion I sustained at the same time.

Among the many people who have influenced me greatly in my life, one stands above them all in so many ways. John Peake was my housemaster for my five years at Eton. He was my teacher, tutor, confidant, sports coach and general morale booster. He exhibited that particular ability to always be himself in all aspects of life and work. He and his wife Sue gave me so many life skills. After school, inevitably, we stayed in touch. As a teacher, he imbued in me the love of history, which I applied in the making of my World War II documentary film and book, *The Last Ring Home*. And in *You Lead*, there is a kernel that was sparked by his example.

For *You Lead*, I was fortunate to be able to interview and draw on many wonderfully talented individuals, several of whom I worked with at Redken. It's lovely to know that the friendships I made at work can endure, even grow, through time and despite the distance. Technology has no doubt helped keep those relationships alive.

The list of advisers and helpers are, in alphabetical order: Chris Baran, Jeremy Basset, Alex Beaussier, Tariq Hassan, Peter Mahoney, Ann Mincey, Pat Parenty, Christine Schuster, Adrian Swinscoe, Phillip Ullmann and Laura Willis.

I have long maintained that I am only as strong as my network. I tend to depend upon some members of my network more than others, especially when it comes to writing. Then there are the friends and family who are able to cajole and inspire. I am forever grateful for the unconditional love and support of my father, mother and sister. There is no one more important than my incandescently beautiful and smart wife, Yendi. Between coddling and prodding, encouraging and exhorting, and laughing and loving, Yendi has been the guiding rock by my side for 25 years of marriage.

PART ONE

Setting the stage

The wake-up call for a new form of leadership

My wake-up call happened one gorgeous late summer morning. I was fretting about the upcoming annual worldwide meeting, where all the most senior executives assemble to hear about each brand's panier of new products and planned marketing support to warrant the budgets for the next three years. My New York City-based team was kicking into top gear in the mad scramble before we all had to fly to Paris. I was sitting at my desk in my 19th-storey corner office in midtown Manhattan. The phone rang. I picked it up. And, at the same time, I glanced over my shoulder to the right. About four miles away, with a crystal-clear view, I saw a ball of flame. It didn't seem so large, but it was certainly visible. I hung up the phone and stood up. Smoke was billowing. I called in my assistant, Mary Ann, who without missing a beat, warned that it must be a terrorist attack. Within 10 minutes, pretty much everyone on the floor had swarmed into my office as it was the only one with a view of the World Trade Center towers. The chatter was nervous, subdued. I turned on a local radio station. There was talk of a small passenger plane. Everyone dispersed and I called Paris for a short chat with my boss. I told him about the explosion. As soon as the call ended, I stood up and looked out on the bustling cityscape. I took a couple of zoomed-in photographs of the burning building. I was numbed in part by the distance and distracted by the issues surrounding the meeting preparations.

I have kept with me a vivid but inaccurate recollection of what happened next. Uptown, I thought I spotted a plane, flying down the length of the city. Maybe it was a Canadair coming to extinguish the fire raging on the upper floors of the tower? My attention stayed glued on this plane. I imagined the skilled manoeuvre needed to dump water at that speed, at that height. The plane headed straight for the smoking aperture, then suddenly banked right and dipped out of view. Some 30 seconds later, to my horror, there was another ball of flames engulfing the middle of the south tower. Reality grabbed hold. One penetrating thought struck me: How would my grandfather, the man I'd been named after, have reacted under these circumstances? A US Navy officer, married with a young boy and a girl, he'd been shipped out to the Philippines in the summer of 1941. In the earliest hours of 8 December 1941, as captain of the USS Napa anchored in Manila Bay, he had written in the margin of the ship's logbook, '0340 hours. Received word that hostilities with the Japanese Empire had started'. In learning about his abbreviated life, I began to take stock of my own past, my own character and connecting with what was most important.[1]

In the five hours that followed, I had an electroshock that continues to reverberate today. It made me start to question: What am I really doing that matters? As the years progressed, I came to understand how much my personal life was intertwined with my professional career. We are indeed fashioned by our real-life experiences and it's important to recognize the role of our personal life in the way we develop in business. I went on an invigorating path to be the best version of me both inside and outside the office. I sought to embrace my true self and to merge my personal and professional selves to become one. Yet I've long had a nagging question: Why did I wait to experience a life-changing event in order to change? I am convinced you can find the answer without needing to suffer an electroshock. I'm hoping you will take inspiration from this story to start or complete your own journey.

In the wake of the global Covid-19 pandemic declared in March 2020, with so many people caught rethinking and recon-figuring what's important, it's time for a radically different way to think and act, with a leadership style that is neither currently taught in business schools nor commonly accepted in board-rooms. For those of you who are ready to gear up and lead as you are, welcome aboard. If you needed one last impetus, you may also see positive benefits in your company's valuation. Raj Sisodia and Jag Sheth, co-authors of *Firms of Endearment*,[2] showed that companies led by passion and purpose, so-called *firms of endearment*, significantly outperformed in terms of shareholder return. The firms of endearment featured in their book outperformed the S&P 500 by 14 times over a period of 15 years (1998–2013). These 22 US-based firms even outstripped the 'Good to Great' companies cited in John Collins' celebrated book of the same name by six times over the same period.

But, at the end of the day, as much as I would have you under-stand that the new leadership is a way to perform better, the massively underrated component is that when YOU LEAD as I'll describe, it is far more enlivening and enriching for you on a personal level. And here's the rub: you need to be you. You will need to be honest with yourself, dig into your personal story and accept your whole imperfect self. If you plan to spend anything over 40 hours leading every week, that's 50 per cent of your waking hours in a work week. Thus, it's got be a genuine part of your life and who you are. When YOU LEAD, you'll find the best way to be yourself, get results and the genuine reputation to which you aspire.

What makes this era fundamentally different from the past is that the pace and volatility are now happening increasingly in the open. We, as leaders, are deluged by new questions, choices and exogenous forces and need to respond in real time, in plain view. Trust, the true currency of leaders, is sorely lacking. There is no prior roadmap to help us navigate through the change. The laws that govern the World Wide Web (aka the Wild West World) are systematically in arrears, requiring us to bring to the fore our own ethical backbone – which is by definition personal – as we decide about the new opportunities and usages of these new technologies. In this context, as an executive you will need to adapt to a new form of leadership, one where you'll need to fix your personal 'North Star' setting and create your own moral compass. Being courageous enough to share both with your team will help you to chart your path, make the tough decisions and guide you ethically, often in uncharted waters. You'll learn why and how to lead from the centre, where you bring your whole self to work, day in and day out. You'll accept your own vulnerabilities and embrace the messiness of personal relationships. *You Lead* is, at heart, about human-first leadership. This will start with yourself, course through your employees and partners, benefit the customer, and thence the bottom line.

When YOU LEAD, you'll find the best way to be yourself, get results and the genuine reputation to which you aspire.

In *You Lead*, I've laid out how to construct your guiding principles and navigate a path through these disruptive times with the aim of crafting long-term success and accomplishment at the same time as developing a sense of personal fulfilment.

Endnotes

1. Lt Minter Dial, USN, was the decorated captain of the USS Napa, a World War I tugboat, stationed in the Philippines when the war broke out. In what seemed like an eerily similar surprise attack, at Pearl Harbor, 2,403 service members died. On 9/11, 2,606 people were killed in the World Trade Center and surrounding area. (A total of 2,996 people were killed that day, including the airplane passengers, in the four separate incidents.) His life story is the subject of a book and documentary film, shown on History Channel and PBS, called *The Last Ring Home* (www.thelastringhome.com (archived at https://perma.cc/Z33M-ZPM2)).
2. Sisodia, R and Sheth, J (2014) *Firms of Endearment: How world-class companies profit from passion and purpose*, Pearson FT Press, www.firmsofendearment.com/ (archived at https://perma.cc/2SRK-JRPM)

CHAPTER ONE

It's a rocky world

CHAPTER OVERVIEW

As the winds of change continue to whirl at pace, it's easy to get knocked off course. Leaders need to find a way to navigate through often countervailing forces by having the courage to develop a personal and ethical voice. They must define what they stand for in themselves, with their employees and the brand's stakeholders. The transformation that leaders must make in these turbulent times is less about which new technologies to use and more about having right mindset.

Making values come alive

One of the most important and disruptive shifts in business with the wave of new technologies, ranging from smartphones to social media to 5G to artificial intelligence (AI), has been the way we communicate. Many of these technologies directly impact our communications. Moreover, the way we live and communicate outside of work is materially important for the way we work in business. This became patently clear during the Covid-19 pandemic lockdown where so many of us were thrust into working remotely from home. Our personal and professional worlds all of a sudden – even if it was because of an exogenous force – became intertwined. The notion of putting up a wall between our personal and professional lives is not just outdated. It's the quickest way to lose the plot. This doesn't just mean the ability to stay on top of the goings-on inside the company. It's about staying in touch with the lives of the employees and, crucially, how the real world operates and how your customers are living and consuming. As many of us came to realize during the lockdown, you couldn't just jump into a work conversation without first checking in on the personal side. This behaviour was lost well before the pandemic set in. In its aftermath, many will inevitably return to their old ways. But the ones who can allow for personal moments in the professional setting will learn to communicate in a far more effective manner.

New to those who discovered remote work during the pandemic, when working in a distributed manner communications become ever more important because of the lack of spontaneous informal chats that one might have in the corridor or at the watercooler at the office. We realized how, by connecting in with each other's context, we were able to create a more profound communication. For remote work to really work, communication style and practice become primordial considerations. And building trust is the critical glue to keep the workflow and outputs effective.

Meanwhile, those of you who keep hundreds of unread messages at a time are in real danger of losing the thread. Those hundreds will soon turn into thousands. And within those unread and unanswered messages will be potential customers, customer feedback, key information for decision-taking as well as key employee issues. There may even be meaningful messages from loved ones. If that's acceptable to you as a leader, then you're setting a poor example for the rest of your team. Don't think that they won't notice at one point the red badge on top of your messages and mail icons.

I'm a steadfast proponent of being responsible for managing one's own communications and setting the proper example. However, there's always the awkward situation where your boss is the one who has the red badge indicating hundreds of unread messages. In such circumstances, you'll have to apply your skills of managing up. Your boss may be in need of some communication skills training to help manage the inbox of the various apps, including adjusting the settings and notifications. Pragmatically speaking, the best thing to do is to ask which the preferred channel is to reach him/her for important messages.

Bringing yourself to work

When you're working in a business, you necessarily bring with you your experiences and existence outside of the office. To ignore them is folly. I remember very well the feeling I had when a boss of mine told me that he was only ever interested in matters that involved work. Not only was I disconcerted, his attitude significantly cut down my trust factor in him. He came off as a cold machine. The issue today is that what happens in real life bleeds into what happens in the office and, similarly, what happens offline impacts online. You don't need to look further than how well you sleep to know that your out-of-office life can impact your productivity at work. But, with the speed of change and constant innovation happening around us, it's important for us all to be aware of the changing habits, options and opportunities that are being crafted in all manner of industries and sectors. These new usages and practices can be entirely relevant to the customer experiences you are hoping to create.

I don't know about you, but unless I'm in a Spring 2020 pandemic lockdown, hardly a week passes when I don't take an Uber or Lyft. In keeping with the modern ways, I don't own a car. I read a personalized newsfeed on Flipboard, digest the best-curated articles via Feedly and am reading nearly all of my books on my Kindle or via Audible. I will regularly ask Siri to operate my smarter-and-smarter iPhone. I'm doing well over 50 per cent of my non-grocery shopping on Amazon. I'm making payments with an array of online-only systems such as PayPal, Starling Bank or Monzo. I am buying coffee at a local café with Bitcoins. I'm finding tennis partners on OpenPartners, dog walkers on Pawshake and a handyman on RatedPeople. For fashion, I've signed up with all my sizes at Bonobos, the online fashion store for men, bought by Walmart in 2017, that provides In Real Life (IRL) fitting services with advice from *with-it* women. I'm running my home via Amazon's Alexa and staying at Airbnbs on weekend getaways. The list goes on... differently for everyone, according to his/her needs, habits and circles. There are new services being conceived and launched daily. The key is that these activities and behaviours have a knock-on effect on my expectations and understanding of what's possible. And I consciously need to bring those experiences and options with me to work.

A leader who isn't immersed in using and staying abreast of these technologies will not be able to relate to the employee or customer experience. For this reason, a leader has to become digital him- or herself. It's not sufficient to be well read on the topic. And it's just not effective to delegate one's communications. When a marketing manager for a large consumer brand once told me that he didn't have time to use social media, I argued that he was in effect saying that he didn't have time to listen to his clients. The way you spend your time is a choice. And, even if it may be challenging to sort out the channels, much less the useful kernels from the sheer volume of noise, there are effective and efficient manners of being social, even at the highest levels. And, yes, it takes time to get up to speed on them and to set up an appropriately curated list of sources. But that's part of the process.

I provide, as a standout example, an individual who is no digital native or Silicon Valley start-up entrepreneur, but a chief executive in a large organization with many millions of customers. Ronan Dunne is the CEO of the Verizon Consumer Group and a self-described Chief Storyteller. He's also a regular Twitter user (@RonanDunneVZ) and has said on many occasions that he uses Twitter to listen directly to what people are saying about his business. He describes it as a way to walk down the shop-floor aisles and listen to what is really going on, as opposed to the muffled lines of communication that typically happen inside the boardroom. Moreover, by using Twitter for 15 minutes in the morning, Dunne has an ear in the field, limited though he knows it is, that allows him to discourage the attitude among his direct reports of telling him what they *think* he wants to hear. Furthermore, by being active on this channel, he has become accustomed to the vernacular and is directly familiar with its benefits and pitfalls.

One last point about Dunne's presence on Twitter that is noteworthy: he presents a complete picture of himself that is personal, yet professional. Specifically, he is unafraid to announce his patriotic support for the Irish rugby team. Where some might be concerned about offending others, Dunne wears his colours on his sleeve. He incarnates the idea that you're better off being you than, for example, pretending to like everything in the same way all the time. By setting the example, Dunne is also encouraging his team and all employees under him to participate online. Of course, there must be guidelines and a degree of training; and there will always be the occasional mistake. Yet, by encouraging his team to be fluent online, he is mobilizing a very large group of potential influencers. And he won't be easily duped by his advertising agency into spending money on institutional campaigns that are tone inappropriate.

The employee as evangelist

The 'social employee', as written about in the eponymous book by Cheryl and Mark Burgess, is a very special concept that cannot be injected into any culture without due preparation and work.[1] Ultimately, the best social employee feels as if the work about which they are chatting is merely an extension of their personal values, personality and, even, identity. This is why the thorny and highly tendentious issue of politics at work is becoming more common. Especially when the political issues are directly related to the industry in which you work, it is increasingly difficult for executives to skirt or duck the politics. But it's also important to gauge how much your employees, key stakeholders and customers feel about the political issues. Not that one should always cave in to the demands of these stakeholders, but not coming out with a stance can be seen as quiet acquiescence. When an executive boldly expresses their opinion on political issues, it necessarily comes with risks. This is where having a strong understanding of your core market is crucial. Issues such as climate change, inequality or LGBT rights will over-index as concerns for the younger generations. We have seen numerous high stakes and controversial choices made by big name brands. For example, there was Nike's stand with Colin Kaepernick, the NFL quarterback who was fired after kneeling during the singing of the US national anthem, as a protest against police racism. It was a courageous decision by Nike's leadership that was bound to polarize people, including many customers. Aside from the collateral free press coverage around this polemic decision, the move evidently catered to and pleased a large core group of Nike fans. Sales have been solid in the aftermath. Less talked about, but equally (if not more) powerful, is the rallying cry around Nike by other up-and-coming athletes. Not that stock price performance can be directly attributed to the Kaepernick decision (September 2018), but Nike shares have done well. Since October 2017, at the time of writing they've massively outperformed the S&P500. What I particularly appreciate about Nike's decision is that it was based more on culture and values than on a hardcore mathematical equation. They showed that they were not afraid to stand for something, even if it meant taking a knee. They put their money where their mouth is. Love it or hate it, they took a stand. The Kaepernick mantra, under a Nike swoosh, is meaningful and real to its core:

Believe in something. Even if it means sacrificing everything.

It's proof that Nike just did it. Importantly, in this instance, there is a very real link between Kaepernick and Nike's core business. Aristotle said in his work *Politics* that human beings are by their nature political animals. By taking a political stance that is aligned with your values and resonates with your staff and core stakeholders, the chances of a good payoff increase.

But getting a financial return ought not to be the motivating factor. Don't take this example as a sweeping declaration that all brands must be political. I absolutely advise due caution. First and foremost, the political issue must have relevance for the brand. Second, the senior team must be fully and genuinely engaged. It stands to reason that if the brand has yet to work out its values and what it stands for, it's best to do that homework before launching into the potentially controversial political agenda. Political stances that are merely virtue signalling or aren't in line with the leader's personal convictions are more likely to fall flat if not foul. During the Black Lives Matter (BLM) protests, we saw many brands declare their support, yet they had never made any public declarations previously. Furthermore, some of these same companies seemed only to be paying lip service to diversity and inclusion. As a result, they got called out for their hypocrisy, including by their own employees. Whereas Nike was solidly on brand, its competitor Adidas was caught out for having a distinctly underrepresented workforce, with just 4.5 per cent of its 1,700 employees in its US headquarters who identified as black.[2]

It behoves leaders today to stand up for what's right before it becomes an issue.

It behoves leaders today to stand up for what's right before it becomes an issue. Words won't suffice. Furthermore, having the courage to show your colours (ie act) is likely to galvanize your team. In an exclusive interview I had with Latia Curry, Principal at the communications agency RALLY, she said that:

> social and political issues actually allow for you to connect with people on an emotional level, creating an affinity for you and your brand that can last, in terms of loyalty, for a long time.[3]

Here's a short guide to taking a political stand for your brand.

Guide to taking a political stand

If you're considering taking a political stance, here are the five steps you should take:

1 To the extent you've done your homework and your brand vision and values are well defined, evaluate which issues – ethical and political – align with your company's position. Limit your position to a specific issue. Make sure to do due diligence if you're hooking up with a particular individual, and don't sign up with a political party. Political parties have agendas that change, and they cannot and will not faithfully align with your company's long-term objectives and values.

2 Pick one or two issues in which you are prepared to invest not just time and money but where you are looking to create impact and hopefully encourage, if not instil, change.

3 Ensure that the senior team and the wider employee base are on board and craft some policy statements and guidelines that are systematically shared throughout the organization. In general, you as the leader ought to be prepared to communicate personally and widely on these issues.

4 Start by testing the waters. For example, this can take the form of expressing an opinion in an internal company meeting. This can also be with the next layer of important stakeholders on the front line (eg distributors, sales team).

5 At all times, make sure to be extremely attentive to the ongoing climate and how your activities are being appreciated. As Curry stressed, it's important to develop a voice and avoid being tone deaf to the wider audience's cares and opinions.

When an employee is allowed to bring their full personality to work, the power and amplification of the social employee takes on another level. When an employee feels empowered to talk about the brand for which they are working, it is contributing to and reinforcing their personal brand. With a more evolved mindset, senior management (and human resources teams) should consider helping their employees to develop their own personal brand. For if personal affairs are systematically left at home and the professional life is squirrelled away at the office, the enterprise is bound to operate at a fraction of its effectiveness.

A brand whose values resonate with its employees on a personal level is bound to make for stronger convictions, a more engaged sponsor and, ultimately, a stronger customer relationship.

The employee as consumer

Another divide that is equally important from a business perspective is between employees and customers. Developing empathy and an ability to think as and for your customer is becoming ever more vital. Every employee is a consumer outside of the office. But many employees (especially when they become senior managers) come to work and, while slipping on the corporate suit, seem to leave behind their lives as consumers. The excuse may be the pressure on results and the quest for shareholder return, yet it is precisely the experience of and empathy with the customer that will make the difference longer term.

Companies and cultures that privilege the 'rational' and 'financial' drivers of the business will undoubtedly struggle to adopt a customer-centric attitude. As it is, CEOs and top management are already cut off from the 'reality' of the customer experience by spending obscene amounts of time behind closed doors and in meetings. When they do customer 'meet and greets' or store visits, their experience is often warped by well-intentioned managers who manicure the floor and present the brand in its best possible light as opposed to the reality. Not that you always want to give the consumer what they *want* (otherwise, we would only be riding faster horses, to paraphrase Henry Ford); but leaders need to embed honest listening into their boardroom. It's up to each company to find its own mechanism, but I like to highlight how Amazon CEO and founder, Jeff Bezos, used the 'trick' of having an empty chair representing the voice of the customer at the table. It's a fine substitute as long as the CEO allows others to invoke the customer in the face of the CEO's wayward suggestion. In the case of Amazon, it makes consummate sense in that its vision statement is to be 'the Earth's most customer-centric company'.[4] Obviously, Bezos' personal dedication to this concept helps to make the presence of the chair come alive. The chair's just a tool. Like all tools, its effectiveness depends on how it is used.

Branding is personal

In the business-to-consumer (B2C) world, customers are looking for a different kind of relationship with brands. Naturally, a customer of a laundry detergent is not expecting the brand to come and join the family for the Sunday roast. We aren't always searching for a relationship with a brand. But expectations are such that consumers are looking for more than just a good product. At a minimum, they consider the surrounding service, before, during and after purchase, as part of the brand experience. Thanks to the multiplicity of digital tools and platforms, each brand has more opportunities to connect with its customers, to gain permission to exchange with them and to earn their trust. And it's done at a personal level. Consumers – and employees of these very same brands – are 'unliking' brands whose values are not sufficiently relevant, strong or believable. Customers' consumption habits have changed. Rocked by wave after wave of bad news and worries – including economic woes, political doubts, potential terrorist attacks, man-made as well as natural catastrophes – layered in with the transformational effects of the internet, the consumer's world has been structurally shaken.

Meanwhile, people in the business-to-business (B2B) world, while different in many aspects from B2C, put even more emphasis on trust. I still hear B2B executives suggest that social media has no role to play in their world. I disagree. B2B is inherently more about relationships. There are plenty, if not more diverse, ways to use social media to generate leads, convert business and enhance loyalty. A great example is LinkedIn's Marketing Solutions Blog.[5] Designed for B2B marketers, the blog is rich in great content.

Among the major consultancies, Deloitte created a video for its Global Impact Report in which the company affirms its purpose: 'We believe that we must use our resources to make a positive impact on the world.'[6] In this case, the video is targeted at its employees, future recruits and potential customers. It's the kind of message that resonates on a more personal level. Even if the video is a bit too polished for my liking and has just 13,000 views, it shows that even in the driest of industries, social media can serve a useful purpose. As an important aside, one should judge the success of an effort based on the achievement of an intended objective, not on the vanity of the numbers.

If the new digital platforms and tools have an impact on every area of the business, the disruption in branding and marketing is especially important for leaders to get their heads around. In large part that is because there is no easy recipe to follow. What worked yesterday will systematically fail tomorrow if the appropriate learnings haven't been made and integrated into the new programme or campaign. In matters of branding, a lot has changed over the last decade because of two important factors. First is the resistance to BS. Overall, trust levels in corporate and marketing communications are low – and for the most part with good reason – because of an overdose of manicured and deceitful messages. In French, the terminology *faire de la comm* means de facto to manage the narrative, aka propaganda. A tweet that comes from the corporate Twitter account typically carries more weight if it has someone's personal initials as a sign-off. Not only does it humanize the company, it's a sign of accountability. Of course, better yet, it's most credible when it comes from an individual's account, complete with an appropriately filled-in profile.

The second and related factor is our latent desire for meaningfulness and a corresponding intolerance of inauthenticity. There is a major cleavage under way between value-added brands and the no-frills inexpensive brands. Brands and products positioned in the middle are, by definition, a compromise and risk getting lost in the fray. Aside from the revolution caused by the tsunami of new technologies, we've seen a large number of middle-of-the-road brands suffer or fail for a lack of distinction, positioning or conviction. Not only are we all more aware of or educated about the improprieties of brands, we are seeking more fulfilment out of the brands on which we spend our hard-earned money. We increasingly look at the brands we buy as a viable way to reaffirm our own set of values and identity. Brands whose promises are broken or don't ring true are increasingly rejected. Every category now has a reasonable unbranded or cheap alternative available, for example, at hard discounters.

The brand problem is accentuated by technology. It is now easy to see and compare inconsistencies in brand messages, thanks to the power of the Google search engine. And it's inadvisable to issue corporate messages (whose destined audience is typically the shareholder) that are incoherent with either commercial or employer brand messages. Not only are all these messages visible to the public online, the employee has a view of all such messages as well. As a result, it stands to reason that inconsistencies – that attempt to mask or manage the real meaning – will have a negative impact on employee engagement.

The evolution of branding

The notion of branding, thus, has materially changed and requires leaders to operate in a different manner. Specifically, and in response to customer trends, brands need to find ways to engage authentically and at scale. Customers don't care for spam; they want personalization. Institutional, impersonal messages are mistrusted. There are now many more touchpoints, enabled through technology, allowing for many more interactions along the customer journey with different individuals in the brand. These individuals are participating in creating a delightful customer experience that can't be dictated through rigid policies and processes.

And on the inside, with the heated competition for talent, employees seek fulfilment and a sense of belonging with a brand whose culture and values resonate. As a leader, in order to tap into the employees' discretionary energy and create greater engagement, you'll need to craft an environment that truly touches the team at a deeper level, day in and day out. You'll need to earn their trust and to demonstrate the behaviour you want to see happen throughout the organization. You'll need to encourage your teams to push the boundaries, collaborate, experiment and overcome their fears. To make your brand come alive every day, you'll want your employees to be your brand's number one fans and advocates. As we'll explore later, you'll want them to bring their whole selves to the table. Everything converges on one important message: branding must get personal. As an executive, we need to allow for our personal spheres to merge into the professional and remember that we are at once consumer and worker (see Figure 1.1).

FIGURE 1.1 Embracing the divide between professional and personal spheres

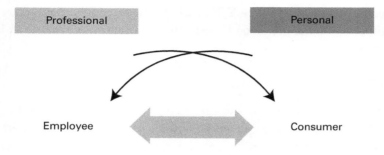

Scaling the digital mountain

As we roll into the third decade of the 21st century, every executive team has had to undergo some form of transformation. There can't be many companies left that haven't awoken to the reality that the new technologies are having an impact on their way of functioning, no matter the industry. Notably, these new technologies have changed communications and the customer relationship. They've also materially changed the options in operations and, in many cases, the business model. Whether or not it's been under the guise of a specific digital transformation programme, executive teams have matured. At some level, we should stop calling these technologies *new*. Digital transformation will evolve to drop the word digital, and programmes will merely convert into business as usual. Yet, the vast majority of companies have only scratched the surface of what these technologies can provide. There are many more technological innovations to come, avenues to explore and new usages still to be uncovered. Thus, transformation is not a destination but a journey, and the road ahead will remain paved with new challenges. As fast as the dust settles on an initiative, there'll be a new storm brewing around the corner. Executives barely ever give themselves the time to decompress and digest the true lessons learned from their past efforts or errors, which will leave them prone. **When YOU LEAD, you will allocate sufficient time to understand and learn from your experiences and experiments.**

The mountain of opportunities

New technology offers the executive a plethora of options. For the most part, these can be viewed as opportunities. But there are plenty of risks and threats interposed among them. I liken the situation to a climber faced with an unscaled mountain, as shown in Figure 1.2. It's a digital mountain with obstacles and overhanging issues. Among the myriad choices, which path to choose? There are many concepts and layers that will nuance the choices and need to be taken into consideration, between the more dangerous challenge of security and the manifold ways of using artificial intelligence, to the need to operate in real time, with an always-on system. Between the onslaught of new tools and platforms and the multitude of new acronyms and foreign concepts, it is very easy to become disoriented. Without allowing the time for exploration and due consideration, it's difficult to take full stock of the options and impacts. The secret to finding your path up the mountain lies in how you tie in with your strategy. By having a clear strategy that is shared throughout your team, you will be better able to orient your selections and apply your resources.

By having a clear strategy that is shared throughout your team, you will be better able to orient your selections and apply your resources.

Importantly, many people will underestimate the requisite change in operation in order to take advantage of it. That's because the change means tackling the business's culture. And that requires adjusting the mindset. Hopefully, with this book, you will be better equipped to tackle the change.

FIGURE 1.2 Scalling the digital mountain

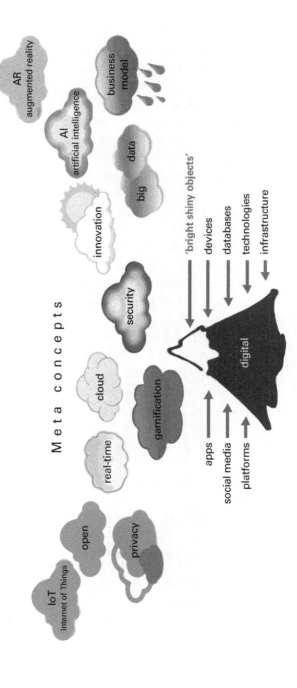

The size of the task can create an enormous disturbance because the 'digital transformation project' is inevitably done in addition to keeping the business running. One needs to embrace the new tech all the while making sure that the current business isn't upended. It's like the integration of a new e-commerce platform or an upgrade in financial accounting software. There is a need for beta-testing in parallel to keeping the business humming. Then, when it comes to flipping the switch, it's all about making sure the shutdown is as short as possible and that the new interface or program is working smoothly. In a digital world, however, it's not about if but *when* there are bugs. Not only are senior executives blithely unaware of these under-the-hood challenges, the risk is to focus on parsing out blame rather than learning the true underlying lessons. As important as digital has become, it is not a strategy in itself, nor is it something that can be delegated to an individual. Digital touches all aspects of the business, horizontally and vertically. I wince whenever a company has marked digital transformation as a 'strategic initiative' (or words to that effect). Not only does it give too much weight to the technology, it eschews the need for radical cultural change, starting at the top. Digital by itself isn't strategic. It's a term that broadly represents an array of technological tools, devices and platforms that need to be applied to the company's overall strategy.

Digital, by itself, isn't strategic.

The way a leader articulates the company's strategy is really the vital – and often missing – piece for organizing the digital transformation programme.

Impact on business: how to unlearn and rewire

As companies tackle the digital opportunities, the challenge inevitably becomes one of organization and culture around one central question:

To what extent are we prepared to render an excellent customer experience?

There are questions of process and infrastructure that are absolutely fundamental to the equation. However, leadership teams cannot take refuge behind substantially rational questions and ought to focus first and foremost on the people, their mind-set and behaviours. The need is to figure out the 'old' habits that must be broken or 'unlearned' as Jack Uldrich, Chief Unlearning Officer at The School of Unlearning, has often told me in our conversations.[7]

And yet, as much as executives might roll out the mantra that the customer is king and blah-blah-blah, getting focused on the customer journey and experience is only a partial answer, as I'll develop below. At the end of the day, the key to providing exquisite customer service inevitably is through the mobilization of your team. And to get that to happen, you need to embrace a new mindset (which we will cover in depth in Chapter 4).

Revisiting the budget

Among the major hurdles are the limited resources, both financial and human. The finance department is one of the areas where tradition runs thick, and where geekiness and social media netizens are few and far between. In order to 'fit' digital into the workflow and embed it in the organization, there is a need to make strategic choices that help free up time and resources to make the company more agile and to be able to on-board the new tools, platforms and processes. Yet, as is often the case for large businesses, when the budgeting process means comparing last year's profit & loss (P&L) line by line with the prospective new year, the course of change is inevitably being handcuffed. It favours gradual evolution over revolution and reinforces the habit of repeating promotional mechanics on the anniversary of the previous year's activities. The discrete problem with looking at last year's P&L is that it encourages people to worry about sunk costs, including bad bets and an outdated infrastructure. In this fast-changing world, it's important not to get too attached to past investments or bets when the market is moving in another direction. That's what took down Kodak and Borders. Even supposedly savvy companies can be blind-sided. Take Yahoo, which bet the house on banner advertising, or AOL, which failed to move on from its dial-up walled-garden business model. If these latter two companies still exist, they're but a shadow of their past and have certainly lost their independence.

As much as the chief financial officer (CFO) has a mandate for astutely managing the bottom line, it's important that he or she has a good measure of the real business issues. **Rather than increasing or reducing each line by tenths of percentage points, what would your ideal P&L look like if you were to start from scratch?**

What allocations would best accommodate a truly customer-centric and agile organization?

The organization: the end of the chief digital officer

Among the most important areas to revisit – undo to redo – is the way the company is organized. At first, for companies with low levels of digital maturity, there is a natural tendency to label someone as responsible for digital. However, the issue is that one person cannot be held accountable for digital. Aside from the impossibility of understanding the implications of digital at the operational level for every function or staying atop of all that is happening in digital and new technology around the world, digital – and continuous learning – is a layer that needs to be added into all parts of the business. It is thus the responsibility of all parties in the business to identify, own and embed digital themselves. While I understand the temptation to nominate a head of digital, the more digitally mature companies will know that digital belongs to all. A company that still has a chief digital officer is only signalling its digital tardiness.

Human resources: the right people

People will naturally talk about digital transformation and change management in the same breath. The issue is that, in this context, change management sounds like a project. Part of any attempt to 'digitalize' a business means ensuring that the right people are in place or, at least, part of the network. In my experience, if a company does not do a satisfactory audit upfront, there is a much greater likelihood of failure or, at least, ineffectiveness. Having the right people, in terms of competencies and capabilities, is one part of it; but having the right attitude is the more critical part of it. You can always teach new skills. But it's awfully hard to change an attitude. One cannot leave behind in the process the alignment of the HR policies and programmes. Human resources managers not only need to model the right mindset, they must know how to screen for the right attitude. They need to be intricately aware of the operational business challenges. To the extent the difficulty with digital transformation lies in cultural change, HR is the primary screening layer for installing the right mindset among new employees. This means creating an environment where work is meaningful, collaboration is endemic, and individuals take responsibility for their learning, personal branding, cyber-security and their own sense of ethics. HR needs to make sure that the set goals, objectives and compensation are adapted accordingly, strategically supporting the business.

The right 'why' is the biggest motivation tool

Riding high above the digital transformation process and the motivation to tackle 'the digital mountain' is making sure that the organization is aligned behind a strong and shared purpose. At the very minimum, this should involve satisfying the customer in a comprehensive manner. At its best, it involves feeling that, as a group, you can make a material difference, not just to the bottom line but also to all your stakeholders. Finding a higher purpose in the digital transformation can become the true golden opportunity. It's a big ask, but it is the real question. We'll get to how to make that happen in Chapter 5.

Recap of key messages and actionable points

- What story we tell, how we tell it and where we do so are fundamental to the ability to mobilize the teams, relate with and to customers, and engage the broader stakeholders.
- It behoves leaders today to know to stand up for what's right before it becomes an issue.
- A brand whose values resonate with its employees on a personal level is bound to make for stronger convictions, a more engaged sponsor and, ultimately, a stronger customer relationship.
- Ideally, you want your team to take their work to heart. In other words, that they take it personally.
- Ensure you allocate sufficient time to understand and learn from your experiences and experiments.
- By having a clear strategy that is shared throughout your team, you will be better able to orient your selections and apply your resources.
- Digital, by itself, isn't strategic. It's an array of technological tools, devices and platforms that need to be applied to the company's overall strategy.
- Rather than increasing or reducing each line by tenths of percentage points, what would your ideal P&L look like if you were to start from scratch?

Endnotes

1. Burgess, C and Burgess, M (2013) *The Social Employee: How great companies make social media work*, McGraw-Hill
2. www.nytimes.com/2019/06/19/business/adidas-diversity-employees.html (archived at https://perma.cc/VS95-G9Y2)
3. www.minterdial.com/2018/09/latia-curry-rally/ (archived at https://perma.cc/MB2Z-E6EN)
4. www.amazon.jobs/en/working/working-amazon (archived at https://perma.cc/MF2X-SYEB)
5. business.linkedin.com/marketing-solutions/blog# (archived at https://perma.cc/3S8N-56LX)
6. youtu.be/26vzBwSBlJY (archived at https://perma.cc/5JEE-34UG)
7. The School of Unlearning, schoolofunlearning.org/ (archived at https://perma.cc/CV6R-TVWM)

CHAPTER TWO

Got the right governance, Guv'nor?

CHAPTER OVERVIEW

Being yourself in business is easier said than done. Not only does it take knowing yourself, it also needs to work at work. The type of company, its ownership structure, governance principles and culture will have a significant role in curtailing or freeing its leaders in terms of beliefs, behaviours and language. Being yourself means being true to your values and ethics. Especially when steering through tricky issues such as politics, privacy rights and calls for increased transparency, you'll need to take stock of the governance model in which you operate, and the options afforded by the owners.

When I was working at L'Oréal or at the investment bank Donaldson, Lufkin & Jenrette (DLJ), I had very different liberties than when I co-founded my own travel agency or now as an independent entrepreneur. Through these different experiences, I became acutely aware of how the corporate structure and presence of the founder impacted the culture and tolerance for deviance. It's like the challenge of bringing diversity, inclusion and equity de facto into the organization. It's not because it's written in the statutes that racism or gender inequity will evaporate. Similarly, the ability for you to bring your whole self to work is most often circumscribed when company culture is too rigid or sacrosanct, where short-term performance pressures dominate or when brands within the portfolio must pay more attention to corporate policies and synergies than serving the customer. There's not one simple recipe, but your room for manoeuvre depends mightily on the overarching governance. It's important to be cognizant of these governance issues as you strive to bring your most authentic self to work.

Staying critical

As we plough through the next decade, it's clear that no company is immune to stumbling, whether it's a market-leading industrial company, a scrappy entrepreneur or even a member of the major tech players, referred to as GAFAM (Google, Apple, Facebook, Amazon and Microsoft) or in China, BAT (Baidu, Alibaba and Tencent). For example, I recall how the chief marketing officer (CMO) of a large online retailer told me that the solution to a declining email open rate was to add another email to the weekly schedule. In another instance, a CEO for an online travel company kept deluding himself that their less-than-ethical approach to pricing (which involved showing one price at the outset and surreptitiously bumping it up with hidden costs at the checkout) was acceptable because others in the industry did the same. In the first case, the individual failed to understand that it

Stay critical and exigent about how you are creating value for your customers and your business.

wasn't about the open rate falling from 2 per cent to 1.8 per cent. It was that there were 98.2 per cent of recipients who found zero (possibly negative) value in their emails. In the second case, the CEO was banking on subterfuge and opacity; such unethical tenure, in an increasingly transparent world, will inevitably be shown up one day.

You can rely on neither the law, industry standards nor opacity as a way to lead your business. You must stay critical and exigent, using your own moral compass, about how you are creating value for your customers and your business in a responsible manner.

Assessing ownership structure

While we are always beholden to a boss somewhere, it's true that certain leaders have greater degrees of freedom and flexibility than others to do what they truly think is best for creating long-term success. To assess that freedom, I look at ownership structure and governance along three axes, as in Figure 2.1:

1 X axis: What is the relationship between the corporate (umbrella) and commercial brands?
2 Y axis: To what extent is the company publicly traded?
3 Z axis: To what extent is the founding family involved?

Each of these axes exists as a continuum. And there is no absolute prescription as to which is best. However, as we'll explore below, some situations are far better than others. The key is to take stock of how these ownership structures impact (or impede) one's degree of freedom. If you are lucky enough to choose your structure, you are in a privileged position. For most of us, it's a framework we've got to live with.

FIGURE 2.1   Triple axis ownership and governance

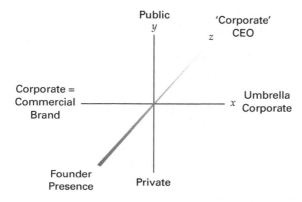

X axis: corporate versus commercial names

The X axis pits the corporate holding company name against the commercially traded names. It's probably the least discussed of the three axes when it comes to leadership. Every company situation is different and comes with a lot of baggage and complexities. And yet it's important to understand the implications it has for the ongoing business in terms of latitude for change, talent management and even resource allocation.

To the extent you naturally have ambitious plans to grow, there are a number of models of growth:

- Like-for-like – where growth is measured by the increase of the existing portfolio of products and services in the same territory.
- Geographic – growth that involves opening up new geographical territories.
- Concentric extensions – where the company creates different brands in the same general category.
- Horizontal extensions – where the company opens up to new categories, on the margin of the core industry.

- Conglomerate diversification – also known as opportunism, this is where acquisitions are made in new territories that share no technological or commercial links or similarities.

Of course, there's always the other phenomenon where you end up dissolving, being acquired or having to sell. But let's just say that's for another day.

As your company expands, you'll need to consider carefully the options and avenues for growth. On balance, there is nothing better than organic, self-funded growth. That's because you are showing an innate ability to grow what you already own. But that's not eternally possible, no matter the business. Industries *always* evolve and mature. What course of growth will you pursue? For some choices, it's a classic case of easy come, easy go. For example, when looking at geographical expansion, there's the option of opening up territories with distributors, wholesalers or franchisees as opposed to wholly-owned subsidiaries and/or your own stores. By ceding the operations and/or access to the customer to a third party, it may provide a quick boost to sales, but there is an inevitable loss of control of the brand.

Growth by acquisition

Many companies will look at mergers and acquisitions (M&A) to secure growth or shore up markets. The question then becomes one of brand reach, nomenclature and culture. For example, when you buy a smaller brand, should you keep trading with two different commercial brands and keep the acquiror's corporate name riding above both commercial entities? As a brand guy, who's dead set on the power of the person and personality of the leader to help drive the value of the brand, whenever the corporate name is not the commercially traded brand name, there is a risk of dilution of the brand. Whereas massive conglomerates were all the rage in the 1960s and 1970s, we saw how that bubble burst because of the obvious incoherence of having a financially engineered corporate glue attaching disparate pieces. Growth by acquisition within a specific sector is a totally viable path, but if the acquiror keeps its original name (that's also a commercial name) at the corporate level, it comes with two major risks:

1 The mother ship's brand name will always take a form of preferential treatment, to the extent that the shares' fortunes will be tied up with the commercial success of that brand in the field, versus the success of the acquired brands.
2 The cultural integration of the acquired brands may not succeed (as in the majority of cases).

The failure rate of mergers and acquisitions – at least as gauged as successfully creating long-term shareholder value – is estimated at over 50 per cent.[1] And it's no surprise to me, having seen up close how they are handled. Due diligence, for example, rarely if ever touches on the single biggest issue in my opinion: cultural incompatibilities. And this harkens back to a central but marginalized element addressed in the Business Roundtable's 2019 manifesto.[2] A business's culture is inevitably carried by the many stakeholders. If you don't manage or pay heed to your own culture, much less the one you are acquiring, you will observe first-hand why 'culture eats strategy for breakfast' as business guru, Peter Drucker, purportedly declared.

Here are two important questions to ask yourself:

1 How much of your commercial brand is embedded or allowed into the corporate discourse?
2 How aligned are the communications between the corporate, commercial and employer brands?

When assessing a company culture, I pay particular attention to the notions of 'head office' culture and the operational culture within the subsidiaries. The difference is very much the expression of the corporate brand versus the commercial brand. As on the left-hand side of the X axis, if the corporate brand is the same as the commercially traded brand, there is a far greater coherence and justification for having the same culture through and through. Chanel, Clarins and Apple are illustrations of a unified corporate and commercial identity. Except for a few outlier business units, every item Apple Co. sells carries the Apple logo. Apple employees working on iTunes, iCloud, iPhone or in an Apple store all touch and sell Apple. The most visible exceptions in the Apple portfolio presently include Beats and Shazam; but otherwise, their acquisitions end up being folded into the Apple family.

At the other end of the X axis, when the corporate brand is different from the trading entities it owns, there is a gap that exists between shareholder priorities and commercial issues. For Procter & Gamble, for example, which owns a large and fluid set of brands covering multiple sectors, there is not a single product sold under the brand P&G. In other words, P&G is never on the front of the pack. The same is true of Unilever, Alphabet (the parent of Google) and Kering.

The challenge is considerably more complicated for the companies in the middle of the axis, when the corporate brand is *sometimes* the commercially traded name. I call these the hybrid companies, such as Samsung, L'Oréal, LVMH and Daimler. These are the companies in the middle of the road in Figure 2.2, where the corporate brand's name is shared as part of one or more commercial brands while the remainder of the portfolio of brands trade under different brand names, dissociated from the overall corporate brand name.

Between the Corporate=Commercial and Corporate Umbrella options, the strongest proposition is when the corporate name is also always the commercial name. But naturally that alone doesn't ensure success. To wit: the ongoing successes of hybrid L'Oréal and LVMH. Samsung, which is one of the main competitors of certain parts of Apple's business, has a very different and varied corporate structure. Over the years, Samsung, which is the largest *chaebol* (family-owned conglomerate) in South

FIGURE 2.2   Corporate versus commercial brand names

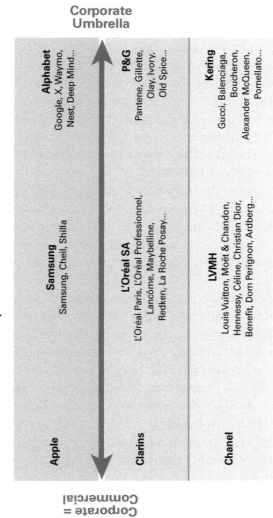

Corporate/Brand Structure

Korea, has accumulated approximately 59 unlisted and 19 listed companies on the Korean stock exchange.[3] It used to have a rather uniform and unified structure, whereby the corporate structure and the commercially traded entities all carried the Samsung name. But it's now divided up into three different entities (Samsung Electronics, Shilla and Cheil), with wildly differing activities. Perhaps this was all part of a master plan of the founder, Lee Byung-chul, since the origin of the word Samsung in Korean is *three stars*. The tripartite structure it seems is essentially to suit the family heirs, so that each of the founder's three children has a business to run. Meanwhile, several of its recent acquisitions, including Harman and Dacor, have been allowed to keep their separate identity.

Yet, despite the disorienting and confusing corporate structure, as seen in Figure 2.3, the performances of Samsung Electronics' (which doesn't include all of the conglomerate's businesses) and Apple's share prices have been remarkably similar over the past five years despite very different leadership styles and company culture.

Driving growth at the scale of companies such as Apple and Samsung is daunting. Despite the confusing and hybrid structure, Samsung continues to be run by the founding family, which ensures continuation of the entrepreneurial spirit. Apple on the other hand has a far more congruent set of business activities, and it also has more complete control of the entire chain of interactions with the customer, including down to its Apple stores. On balance, even if it were easy to buy Samsung shares (it's not), I'm more bullish on Apple's long-term prospects compared with Samsung because of the leadership team, its clear strategy and a meaningful purpose for all who work there.

Among the hybrid examples, for having spent 16 years there, L'Oréal is the business case I know best. The corporate name is L'Oréal SA and the headquarters is based in Paris. On its website, the company cites 46 separate commercially traded names, virtually every one of which, other than the ones that carry the

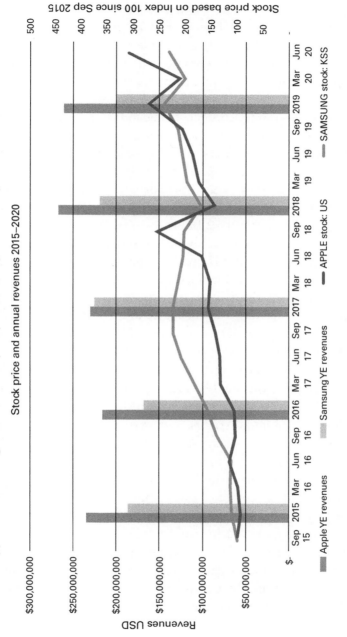

FIGURE 2.3   Apple versus Samsung Electronics stock price performance: June 2015 to June 2020

name L'Oréal on the front, has been acquired, starting with Lancôme in 1964.[4] In fact, beyond those 46, there are other brands under the hood, more or less being consolidated and/or prepared for future expansion. In the matter of sharing the corporate name, there are three commercial entities that use the name L'Oréal as part of their brand name: L'Oréal Paris (mass market division), L'Oréal Professionnel (hairdresser division) and L'Oréal Technique (a smaller entity distributed only in the United States that caters to a wholesaler market). Together these brands probably represent around 15 per cent of the total revenues, but they carry a disproportionately higher brand value, largely by dint of being associated with the parent company. According to the 2019 BrandZ study, the L'Oréal Paris brand alone has a value of $28.4 billion versus a market cap of $165 billion for the entire L'Oréal company at the close of the same year.[5] For hybrid companies, the critical issue is how to sort out and separate the values and the appropriate leadership and personnel between the corporate and commercial entities. The conundrum becomes ever more evident when it comes to the Brand Tattoo test we'll cover in Chapter 5.

One of the key mitigating elements for L'Oréal, which is by far and away the number one player in the cosmetics and beauty care industries, is the presence of the founding family in terms of shareholder voting rights and participation on the board of governors. Up into her 80s, Liliane Bettencourt, the daughter of L'Oréal's founder, Eugène Schueller, had around a 30 per cent stake in the company and was active on the board. Her presence, along with a complex ownership arrangement with Nestlé, helped ward off nationalization and potential suitors. More importantly, she was instrumental in allowing the various CEOs to pursue above-average investments in R&D and marketing, along with a long-term strategy of growth through acquisition. Today, there are three members of the Schueller clan (including through marriage) on the board that has 14 members in total.

Together, these three individuals now control a family stake of around 33 per cent. To the extent that the family is voting on a united basis, L'Oréal will be able to ensure its independence and invest in ways that greedier shareholders might not have approved of. But, as has been widely displayed in the press, that solidarity is far from guaranteed, especially as the generations pass along.

Y axis: publicly traded versus privately held ownership

First, it's worth providing a definition of 'privately held' and 'publicly traded' companies. In the former, at the extreme, these are companies whose ownership is held 100 per cent by the founder or co-founders. Typically (but not necessarily) these are smaller companies. As shown in Figure 2.4, there is a scale of financing through friends/family, into venture capital, and then private equity given in exchange for ownership, yet without these shares being publicly tradable. Despite not being publicly traded, the more the ownership is held by external parties, the more pressure there is on performance commensurate with the ambitions of these stakeholders. When it comes to publicly traded companies, once again, there's a scale. For example, there are some publicly traded companies where holders of the floated stock – and attendant voting rights – are restricted, such that the 'public' can't exercise meaningful pressure. Meanwhile, in the privately held group, I don't include state-owned companies such as the Saudi-owned Aramco.

Access to money – for example, in the capital markets – is, of course, a godsend for companies that need major upfront investments to build out their business infrastructure. But that money comes at a price in the form of accountability and freedom. A privately held company that has self-funded its growth has the flexibility, within the limits of its finances and assuming positive cash flow, to operate with long-term thinking without pandering as much to near-term results. As the ownership and voting rights

FIGURE 2.4   Publicly traded or privately held

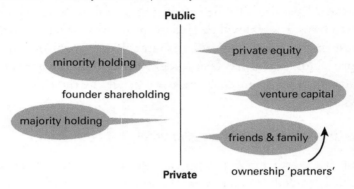

get diluted, so too does the freedom to rule the roost. It's not that shareholder pressure doesn't serve its purpose to make sure a company returns a profit to those who risked investing their money. However, in exchange, the manoeuvring room of the executive team drops off precipitously.

The run-up to The We Company's intended IPO in late 2019 provides a perfect case in point.[6] In a tussle for voting rights in the face of WeWork's unproven business model, the messianic co-founder and CEO, Adam Neumann, first had his wings clipped and then voting rights deeply discounted in hopes of keeping the float alive. In the end, he was summarily removed (albeit with a big payout). In the meantime, the valuation of The We Company has been greatly reduced. Ownership percentage doesn't necessarily indicate voting power. Facebook's co-founder and CEO Mark Zuckerberg and Alphabet's (the umbrella company that owns Google) co-founders Larry Page and Sergei Brin have minority ownership in their respective companies, but they still have proportionately higher voting rights. In the case of Alphabet, the trio of Brin, Page and ex-chairman Eric Schmidt own about 13 per cent of the company and over 50 per cent of the voting rights.[7] Another worthwhile case to show how best to manage a publicly traded company is Amazon. Jeff Bezos, Amazon's founder who is still CEO, now has around a 12 per cent stake in the company and an equivalent voting base.[8] To date, commendably, Bezos has managed to keep the stock market on side thanks to three assets:

1 His performance at the helm of the company has been consistently on or ahead of expectations. Between his 'Day One' attitude,[9] keeping an empty chair in the boardroom to represent the customer,[10] and his unconventional approach to running meetings,[11] Bezos has led a very successful growth strategy that is paying off through a tightly run and well-diversified operation.
2 Bezos has cleverly managed expectations by making his vision clear and aligning shareholders around it: *To build the Earth's most customer-centric organization.*
3 He has been – and still is – the largest single shareholder of Amazon. He's got a great deal of skin in the game and that carries weight in the market, not just because of the sizeable voting rights.

Bezos' mastery of shareholder pressure is genius. The Amazon Leadership Principles as described on its website are uncommonly powerful for their consistent presence throughout the organization.[12] To understand these principles is to get into the mindset of Bezos and, significantly, get under the hood of the Amazon culture.

Meanwhile, private companies with astute management will tend to tenaciously hold on to the privately held status until such time as it is no longer feasible according to their strategic intentions. Without the pressures of short-term performance – which include all the requisite preparations and paperwork to file in addition to the actual numbers falling into place – privately held companies will be freer to manage for the long term. As a direct consequence, the finances are opaque to the outside world, but one may look at the longevity of privately held companies such as Chanel and Mars (among the consumer-facing brands) to see the merit of keeping the shareholders from poking holes in a long-term strategy. Whenever possible, I believe that self-funded growth and private ownership is most desirable. Yet, even privately held companies will always (and should) have short-term tensions and pressures. The key point is that once a company cedes some ownership in exchange for funding, there is an inherent manacle that limits the freedoms for a brand to express itself with independence and personality. This is important to recognize since, as we'll present later in this book, when you lead with your full self, you'll absolutely need to bring the other shareholders and stakeholders on board with you. In any event, whichever your ownership structure, be prepared to tell your brand story over and over again.

Z axis: forging the founding family

The third and final axis relates to the presence of the founding family in leadership. When the founder is a single person or a set of entrepreneurial partners, they inevitably create an initial stamp or DNA for the company. They share an important reason for setting out on a risky venture. Along the way, they encountered challenges, heartaches, trials and tribulations that they dealt with in the best way they knew how. That journey becomes part of the brand story. Even in those organizations that have pivoted multiple times, there remains a trace – however involuntary – of the founders' imprimatur. I love to take the example of Peugeot, where my father worked as a senior executive for over a decade, that went from coffee mills to pepper grinders to automobiles. Whether or not as a leader you seek to evolve the culture of your organization, it's important to keep in mind your roots. For starters, it's great material for crafting your story. More prosaically, you'll need to understand it in order better to manage long-term success in your transformation effort.

Whichever your ownership structure, be prepared to tell your brand story over and over again.

As the entrepreneurial company grows, the presence or role of the founder(s) inevitably changes. Few are the entrepreneurs who are so talented that they are capable of leading their company from humble beginnings to worldwide titans, although there is a conspicuous group of most highly-valued companies whose founders still run the company. In general, though, the skills required vary at every level of growth. A founder's energies, intentions and attention may wane or waver. Furthermore, in family-run businesses, the challenge is often one of transmission. If there are offspring, are they equipped or willing to take over? Do they have the entrepreneurial fibre and hunger? In top-line manner, Figure 2.5 illustrates the way that a founder and/or offspring can participate in the running of the company. On the left-hand side are some of the ways that the founder(s) stays in control and/or remains involved in the decision-making process. To what extent does the original spirit persist to take the types of risks that forged the company's initial success? Has the founder created special voting rights for his/her shareholding to maintain an over-representation and keep more latitude for bold decisions?

On the right-hand side of Figure 2.5 are just some of the different ways in which the spirit of the entrepreneur may stay present in the operations. Are there offspring embedded in the organization? Is the founder's DNA sprinkled in the company culture or present in the corporate name? To what extent is the founder's path part of the company narrative, in corporate and marketing messages? For example, Patagonia founder and chairman Yvon Chouinard continues to champion the brand and have his voice heard in the press, although he's no longer involved in the day-to-day operations.

Unless you *are* the founder, your role as leader is to evaluate how best to perpetuate the story of the company's founder. At whatever level of the organization you are, there should be ways for you to extend the founder's presence, whether or not he/she continues to play an active role.

FIGURE 2.5　Founder family presence

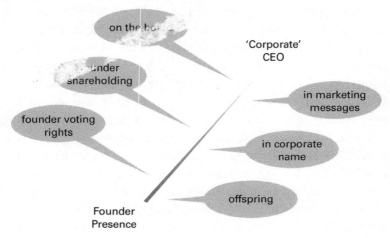

Dealing with transmission

Every successful enterprise will one day need to face the transition away from the founder. It's an important step. It's true that the founder of a start-up is often ill-equipped (or doesn't like) to manage the scale-up process or to run a large and bureaucratic corporation. There is a litany of ways to do so, but one favoured path to transitioning to the next leadership can pass through having the entrepreneur/founder kept on as chairperson. Are there other family members, for example, offspring who you could groom and who would wish to take up the mantle? In any event, the question is: Who will represent the shareholding of the founder as the company grows? This is a truly strategic question in that we're talking about two things: a) the ability for the company to sustain the elements that brought about its initial success; and b) the flexibility and courage to take the hard decisions when the ownership is spread out. When there are too many proverbial cooks in the kitchen, you'll nearly always end up with the equivalent of bangers and mash: ie standard fair. And that is not a tenable long-term position in competitive and volatile markets. So, the question is: How to keep that founding family's entrepreneurial spirit alive? If you're a leader, no matter the size of the company or your position in the hierarchy, you need to participate in keeping the flame of the founder burning.

If I say it's about 'forging' the family founder feeling, I mean both the hardcore notion of casting in metal, as well as the concept of keeping the best possible replica when the founding family has totally moved on (ie a forgery). As head of Redken, within the L'Oréal portfolio, I felt it was my bounden duty to keep Paula Kent Meehan's presence alive within Redken around the world. My great friend and Redken's Global Artistic Director, Chris Baran, assured me that 'the spirit that Paula created is still alive and well within Redken'. A successful brand must be able to live on past the founder. In his interview with me, Phillip Ullmann, founder and chief energizer of the Cordant Group, said, 'Great leaders create leaders and also create self-organizing entities that can fly alone, so it's not just about the leadership. It's the enterprise. If we can create self-governing, self-spawning, self-sustaining enterprises, then we have even more influence.'[13]

> Inasmuch as your organization subscribes to the notion that there are many stakeholders beyond the shareholders, the culture of the company and the personality of the brand depend on the daily interactions. This means how your stakeholders relate and interact together, and how, ultimately, the brand is perceived. Does your brand have a clear set of values that can each be described with specific behaviours?

The bottom line is that certain ownership structures and their attending governance provide far more freedom and flexibility than others. There is no silver bullet because, plenty of times, the founder can be the company's worst enemy (cf Uber's Kalanick or Theranos's Elizabeth Holmes). But, **if I had to prescribe an ideal governance model, it would be a privately held company,**

with a strong presence of the founder family, and to have a corporate name that is also the singular commercially traded brand name.

How to establish an ethical construct

With the plethora of exciting new technological opportunities – be it artificial intelligence to help free up employees from administrative tasks, develop techniques to capture huge amounts of personal data, facial recognition to help profile customers, etc – there are many significant and uncharted waters in which to swim. Ethics count even more now that many of the choices we might make for implementing these technologies have no legal or moral framework on which to base our decisions.

Ethical profit

As I mentioned at the outset, the new manifesto signed by the Business Roundtable members marked a significant shift from the usual dogma of shareholder primacy. It underpins the notion that **profits are the outcome rather than the objective.** Moving away from a pure focus on financial figures and shareholder value and recognizing the value in the many different stakeholders supposes a more inclusive and ethical posture, though not just with suppliers as their memorandum states. In order to put the new manifesto into practice, leaders will need to be particularly attentive to their language and actions. Some companies, such as Patagonia and Harley-Davidson, have been preaching such a modus operandi successfully for many years. The latter described its vision statement several decades ago as:

> Harley-Davidson, Inc is an action-oriented, international company, a leader in its commitment to continuously improve our mutually beneficial relationships with stakeholders (customers, suppliers, employees, shareholders, government and society).[14]

As a consequence, Harley-Davidson has long been operating with the indulgence of the many different partners and stakeholders. In less prosaic terms, its new website states:

> We [at Harley-Davidson] fulfil dreams of personal freedom – it's our purpose, and we take it seriously. And while freedom means different things to different people, it's a bond that brings Harley-Davidson customers, employees, dealers, suppliers and enthusiasts together.[15]

For many hard-nosed companies, run by the finance department, this type of philosophy will be much harder to put in place, because it will typically kowtow to financial considerations. However, as Yvon Chouinard, founder of Patagonia, said:

> Patagonia exists not only to make money, but to prove that it's possible to do the right thing for the planet and still make a profit. After all... there is no business to be done on a dead planet.[16]

Ethics and the value chain

One of the most disruptive opportunities of digital is the ability to break down the value chain. Whichever part of the chain one may be eliminating or dis-intermediating, the 'excess' value becomes profit for the disruptor *and* can be passed along as a more competitive price for the customer. That is marvellous for the end consumer... to a degree. As a brand guy, however, the challenge is making sure that there is value put back into the chain that's left. Notwithstanding the ethics of how the company imposed itself in many markets, Uber leadership made one gross error in managing its value chain. It overlooked the importance of one key component in its value chain: the driver who is literally carrying the Uber brand every trip. Once Uber loses appeal among its driver constituency, the magic of brand Uber will disappear. Its hegemony is built on connecting supply (a critical mass of drivers) and demand (brand recognition on your smartphone). If the drivers feel poorly treated and they spread the news, one passenger at a time, both the supply and demand for Uber will dry up in favour of an alternative offer. If your disruption is merely about extracting value, the brand will be at risk. At its core, brand is a mark of trust and marketing is about creating long-term value.

Ethics are personal

In terms of maintaining your ethical backbone, it is better to have an internal system to uncover unethical practices rather than wait for the laws (or a disgruntled ex-employee or Wikileaks) to straighten out your crooked ways. That requires encouraging your personnel to bring their ethical backbones into the company. Ethics are, by definition, personal. The ethics of your business practice may be hidden from the above hierarchy in the deeper recesses of the organization. These operations, in the bowels of your organization, are being run by middle managers. Do they have a firm grip on a shared ethical framework? Some companies have – or indeed must resort to having – a specific person in charge of ethics in the form of a chief ethics officer.

The more viable long-term solution is to create an ethical framework by which all within the company are held accountable.

Ideally, though, everyone is hired, trained and maintained with a shared set of values and ethics.

Like issues of diversity, sustainable development and, importantly, digital transformation, being ethical is a question of mindset that needs to be shared throughout the organization to be effective. The more viable long-term solution is to create an ethical framework by which all within the company – and especially at the top – are held accountable. If you need to nominate a chief ethics officer, maybe it's a sign you actually have a bigger underlying problem.

Governing data and data transformation

There are many ethical challenges around the ways that new technologies may be brought into an organization. No matter your strategic ambitions, you need to know and communicate how far you're prepared to go to succeed, without relying on laws to provide the lines in the sand. Regulations relating to new tech in many cases won't provide sufficient guidelines. The one sensitive area that will undoubtedly test the ethical boundaries is around how you will approach data. On the one hand, there is an enormous amount of work involved in understanding what data exists, where it is held, how it is gathered, who manages it and who owns it. There are operational questions around data cleanliness, accuracy and compatibility. And then, depending on the country, there are complicated legal questions about permissions and ownership. You'll need to bring your personally informed ethical backbone to the table. You may be compliant, but are your customers going to trust the way you manage the data? To what extent do the employees working on the data ever feel they are compromising their own sense of integrity?

Most data experts, contracted to achieve an expected return on investment, will focus on improving revenues, extracting value and reducing costs. As a rule, they'll be much more tuned into security than they will into privacy. Similarly, the attention will be on compliance rather than on ethics. If you want to earn the trust, you'll need to have genuine empathy for your customers and employees working on and with the data, to create the appropriate ethical construct for how you manage your data.

Data fluency at the leadership level

Companies all have data that is sensitive. Some is in the realm of intellectual property and needs to be kept confidential for competitive reasons. Other data may be sensitive because it contains confidential client information. Too many executives, however, for fear of letting anything out and because they haven't done the requisite triage of sensitive versus non-sensitive information, end up trying to protect *all* their data. That's just an impossible task. The weakest links – typically human in nature – will continue to be exposed. A report published in 2019 by Omnisend stated that there had been 10 billion data breaches in the United States since 2005,[17] and news of more hacks continue to flow in. Recent examples include T-Mobile, where employees' email accounts were compromised,[18] and Microsoft, where 250 million accounts were made vulnerable due to an error (most likely human) in the configuration of security rules.[19] In order to reduce the risk of exposing genuinely sensitive data, each team will need to prioritize the protection levels to allow for the resources to be allocated where they are most needed.

Tomorrow's leaders need to have what I term 'data fluency', where they are capable of discerning and attributing the necessary levels of security to the different types of data. They don't need to be data scientists, but they will surely be better off if they can comfortably understand the difference between structured and unstructured databases, the language and work associated with parsing and cleaning data, not to mention grasping the incredible challenges of getting the best insights and answers from it. The more understanding of data you have as a leader, the more likely it is that you will be able to detect and oversee the ethics involved in managing it. As a starting point, if you have organized a data governance body, make sure there is someone boldly representing the customer's point of view.

Recap of key messages and actionable points

- If you're a leader in a company, no matter its size or your position in the hierarchy, you need to be participating in keeping the flame of the founder burning.

- Inasmuch as your organization subscribes to the notion that there are many stakeholders beyond the shareholders, the culture of the company and the personality of the brand depend on it. This means how your stakeholders act and interact together, and how, ultimately, the brand is perceived. Do you have a clear set of values that can each be described with specific behaviours?
- How much of your commercial brand is embedded or allowed into the corporate discourse? How aligned are the communications between the corporate, commercial and employer brands?
- How to sort out the values (and therefore the attributed personnel) between the corporation and the individual brands?
- Profits are the outcome rather than the objective.
- If your disruption is merely about extracting value, the brand is at risk. At its core, brand is a mark of trust and marketing is about creating value.
- The more viable long-term solution is to create an ethical framework by which all are held accountable.
- You may be compliant, but are your customers going to trust the way you manage the data? To what extent do the employees working on the data ever feel they are compromising their own sense of integrity?
- As much as you might be laser-like in your attempt to extract value, it's critical to remember your personal and corporate values as you work with data.

Endnotes

1. Reed, S and Lajoux, A (1998) *The Art of M&A: A merger acquisition buyout guide*, McGraw-Hill, New York
2. www.businessroundtable.org/business-roundtable-redefines-the-purpose-of-a-corporation-to-promote-an-economy-that-serves-all-americans (archived at https://perma.cc/Z9L3-VA2S)

3. www.hani.co.kr/arti/ENGISSUE/74/472384.html (archived at https://perma.cc/HP2H-ADXM)

4. As of September 2019, there were 46 different brand names listed under BRANDS on its website, www.loreal.com (archived at https://perma.cc/YF5S-ZAKN). This was higher than the number published in its 2018 annual report, which said that L'Oréal had 36 brands, www.loreal-finance.com/system/files/2019-10/LOreal_2018_Annual_Report_0.pdf (archived at https://perma.cc/53AG-F3UN)

5. www.brandz.com/admin/uploads/files/BZ_Global_2019_WPP.pdf (archived at https://perma.cc/XGK3-XD8D)

6. The We Co. is the NY-based parent of WeWork, founded in 2010, that provides shared workspaces for entrepreneurs, small businesses and large enterprises

7. www.investopedia.com/articles/markets/011516/top-5-google-shareholders-goog.asp (archived at https://perma.cc/M7HJ-ZZTN)

8. According to government filings in July 2019, www.yahoo.com/entertainment/jeff-mackenzie-bezos-divvy-amazon-154400398.html (archived at https://perma.cc/SYX8-TPZD)

9. The Day One attitude is Bezos' way of remembering and retaining the scrappy entrepreneurial mindset despite the colossal size of the company. He will systematically attach Amazon's first annual shareholder letter from 1997 to reiterate the mindset the company had at its outset, www.slideshare.net/razinmustafiz/amazon-shareholder-letters-1997-2011 (archived at https://perma.cc/BD9P-XH3L)

10. Bezos famously always brought an empty chair into the board meetings in order to evoke the presence of the customer. It's a practice that is often referred to, but according to certain sources is no longer a prerequisite.

11. Amazon doesn't allow PowerPoint presentations in meetings. Instead, under the policy of the 'Six-Pager', when decisions involve new business opportunities, proposed changes to current operations or are strategic in nature, employees must write a six-page (double-sided) memo that they then read out, word for word, at the meeting. To be sure, it's not always a six-pager, though. For new product launches, the tradition is to write and read a 'PR-FAQ': an internal press release and frequently asked questions, with the answers, of course. For more, check out this article: observer.com/2019/06/amazon-ceo-jeff-bezos-meetings-success-strategy/ (archived at https://perma.cc/28XR-UVNG)

12. Exclusive interview with Phillip Ullmann

13. www.amazon.jobs/en/principles (archived at https://perma.cc/WFY4-UF7X)

14. This is a 1999 archived document from Harley-Davidson that is entitle: 'Doing Business with Harley-Davidson'. www.h-dsn.com/genbus/PublicDocSe rvlet?docID=18&docExt=p (archived at https://perma.cc/FPJ7-JS75)
15. www.harley-davidson.com/gb/en/about-us/company.html (archived at https://perma.cc/KJ6R-M5UU)
16. www.motherearthnews.com/nature-and-environment/patagonia-clothing-zmaz09djzraw.aspx (archived at https://perma.cc/9ZDA-5MCJ)
17. www.omnisend.com/blog/data-breach-report/ (archived at https://perma.cc/74FE-PEVP)
18. www.t-mobile.com/responsibility/consumer-info/pii-notice (archived at https://perma.cc/2NB4-7HCM)
19. https://msrc-blog.microsoft.com/2020/01/22/access-misconfiguration-for-customer-support-database/ (archived at https://perma.cc/D3QQ-AANS)

CHAPTER THREE

Life is work, too

*The test of a first-rate intelligence is the ability to
hold two opposed ideas in mind at the same time and
still retain the ability to function.*
F SCOTT FITZGERALD[1]

CHAPTER OVERVIEW

We'll now explore the fundamental and conflicting issues we face
as human beings and leaders of business. In line with Carl Jung's
Transcendent Function, the acceptance of the tensions between
the opposing forces in our paradoxes will make us grow. While
there are many paradoxes within us, these are four that matter
most in a modern business context. As a leader, you'll want to
apply self-awareness to take stock of how these paradoxes affect
you and your team, and how you plan to navigate your path
through them.

The AND mindset

To manage paradoxes is to accept the dualities that lie within us. I often like to invoke the 'AND Rule' in my executive seminars. Rather than use the word *but*, especially when responding to someone, the AND Rule asks everyone to replace *but* with the word *and*. The sense of direction naturally becomes more positive. Imagine being on the receiving end of these two sentences after having volunteered an idea in a brainstorming session:

Sentence A: 'I hear what you're saying, but I think we can improve it.'

Sentence B: 'I hear what you're saying and I think we can improve it.'

One leaves you feeling diminished, while the second is more positive, right? In Sentence B, the person receiving the comment is much less likely to feel as though their contribution is being discarded.

And the notion of using AND is useful to consider in the new digitized world in which we are operating. When a 'traditional' company is dealing with digital transformation (for example, when leadership wishes to add in new technologies, or drive commerce through the website as opposed to the store, or automate processes in the factory), it should not regard digital as a replacement for offline. You can't just swap digital for analogue on a budget line. Digital isn't something you dictate, especially insofar as the investment in digital may not have an attached revenue stream that warrants the cost. Taking the customer or employee viewpoints, the journey is not digital *or* analogue. It's a dynamic duo. The combination can often be blurred, merged and/or simultaneous. It's sometimes one or the other or both at the same time.

> **KEY INSIGHT**
>
> In terms of effects on your company culture, leadership style and communications, the duality of digital AND analogue needs integrating upstream into all your systems and throughout your processes.

Adopting what I call the AND mindset sets you up better for more complementary thinking and a collaborative spirit. Our lives as leaders are filled with competing tensions, all grasping for our attention. When YOU LEAD, you need to embrace the contradiction of having to be complementary (additional) and decisive (selective). If you can recognize and deal with these paradoxes, you'll be better able to find creative solutions to meet the competing demands. Your role and biggest challenge will be to move out from being underneath the wave of new ideas and options, to grab a strong and strategic North Star setting, to stop being continuously reactive and to be more proactive in the path you cut. This applies notably to the way you position and market yourself as well as your brand.

Charting your North Star setting

One of the absolute *sine qua non* necessities of an excellent leader is to know how to be strategic in your choices. It may sound obvious, but there is much evidence that shows that executives and companies have great difficulties establishing a clear and well-shared strategy. To wit, when I ask senior executives at a company about their strategy in separate interviews, it is not uncommon to hear as many different answers as there are individuals. You might think your strategy is clear, but it's not. A key indicator of the lack of a strong strategy is when it has more than three main bullet points (and they had better be prioritized). With the number of choices growing at pace and coming from different sources and directions, the allocation of our limited resources is more difficult than ever. Consequently, we must be careful in establishing a methodical approach to how we spend our time and energy – including of our team members – to achieve our ambitions. As leader, you need to work on defining your truest North Star, a directional setting that needs to inform all of your important decisions, both personal and professional. In a 2020 leadership survey, fewer than one in four respondents declared that they knew very clearly what their North Star was.[2] Unsurprisingly, only 18.6 per cent said that they felt fully aligned with their North in their lives.

Your North is who you are, not what you do

One of the biggest traps for leaders and businesses alike revolves around how you answer the question: How do you define success? If the answer reposes on items like 'Being number 1 in the market', 'Achieving x per cent growth every year', or on a personal level, 'The title on my business card' or 'The size of my bank account', you're going down a slippery slope that is not only unsustainable, it is empty of meaning. But you can't just wordsmith a definition of success. It has to be something you own, that resonates within and without, and that ideally contributes to others beyond yourself. This is what I consider finding your true North.

When trying to figure out your North, it's important to make it as precise and personal as possible. Ultimately, it should be a phrase that is made-to-fit and belongs to you. If so many people today are busy but bummed out, smiling but burned out, running but going nowhere, befriended by many but close to none, I point the finger at not having a strong North setting. Without a compass, we have a tendency to replace meaning with activity. If you spend the time to characterize your future self and who you want to be, there's a much better chance of achieving that vision.

FIGURE 3.1   Defining your direction in three steps

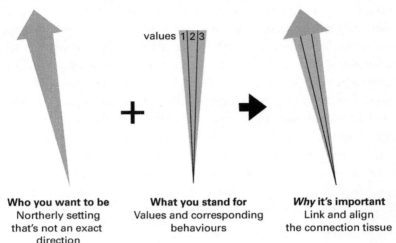

Who you want to be	**What you stand for**	***Why*** **it's important**
Northerly setting that's not an exact direction	Values and corresponding behaviours	Link and align the connection tissue

If not, you'll be running after the wind. As in Figure 3.1, it's better to have a *tight* directional setting than worry about finding an exact North.

So how do you craft a North Star setting? One route is to have someone help you through it, as I did. I was fortunate to have been coached and trained by my mentor, Clément Boyé, in the practice of NEWS Coaching, a brilliant system developed by Aviad Goz. My preferred exercise is to imagine a birthday celebration that's well off (say 15 to 20 years from now). At that party, you invite five important people (alive or dead) in your life, whose opinion matters to you. Each of them toasts you by starting the phrase: 'Happy Birthday! Here's why I cherish you. You're someone who...' And in the following sentence, they express qualities about you. In the aggregate of those five sentences, with a little mining – and providing you're being candid with yourself – you'll find your North. Importantly, this is not a steadfast, dyed-in-the-wool setting. It need not be 100 per cent dead accurate. Avoiding the debilitating ambition of perfection, your North will be a direction that will likely evolve over time.

The second task is to establish what you stand for. These should be expressed as three core values, each qualified with corresponding behaviours as to what those values are and aren't. The work is then crystallized by connecting the values with your North phrase. When your values align with your Northerly setting, you now know *why* it's important to you.

Aligning your personal and professional compass

Being professional and personal need not be a paradox. It certainly shouldn't be a contradiction. You should not be afraid of letting down your guard or mask of professionalism. On the contrary, when YOU LEAD, the real magic happens when your personal North and the North of your business are aligned.[3] In that manner, when you expend your energy, you know why you're burning the midnight oil or sacrificing time on other activities that you might ordinarily have liked to do.

FIGURE 3.2   Aligning personal and professional

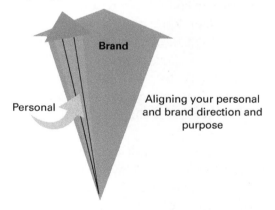

Again, the overlap doesn't have to be 100 per cent, but the more there is an overlap the better. Equally though, when there's little or no overlap, you will want to question why you're working at this particular company. Otherwise, you are spending your limited resources unwisely.

When I accompany executives and senior teams on the journey to crafting a company's purpose or North Star, the biggest handicap and decidedly limiting belief is that one's North must be purely professional. On paper, that might make sense. But the reality is that plans are not executed on paper. They are enacted by human beings with different foibles, issues and motivating forces. When you stay behind the shield of professional ambition, you're not tapping into the most powerful force within us: our emotions. Yes, it's messier and it requires opening up to one's feelings. But the risk of not doing so involves a long list of potential problems, including burnout, apathy, disengagement, absenteeism, accidents and poor morale.

When the world went into lockdown due to the Covid-19 crisis in Spring 2020, many people were thrust into working from home for the first time. It was often an uncomfortable experience, not just because of the lack of equipment and practice at remote working, but also because we were faced with a blurring of the lines between our personal and professional lives. Not a call or message could be started without considering the personal context. Our kids, pets, home décor and ambiance crept into many a Zoom or online video call. As time went along, the polished, image-conscious professional had the veneer pulled off. Through the video calls, CEOs turned into parents, spouses or otherwise individuals with a personal life. Some shone in allowing their authentic personalities to show. Others wilted with the discomfort.

Despite the burgeoning evidence that remote work is an attractive benefit for many employees, it doesn't suit all. And some bosses continue to prefer to have all their employees under their noses. One CEO of a medium-sized financial services company disclosed to me that he'd rather pay a premium to have everyone report into work every day. For leaders who need to control everything, don't trust their employees, aren't comfortable with digital communications, aren't particularly empathic or struggle with transparency, keeping work conditions old school – ie only IRL – may be a better approach. Remote work takes effort, flexibility and appropriate protocols and tools to work effectively.

If remote work is not a solution for all – and for most companies isn't advisable as a dogma – it vividly illustrates why we need to allow our personal selves to be part of our professional experience. Going to work at an office invites people to put on a show, present an image and be seen as industrious. Working from home focuses the mind on results, all the while allowing the worker to be more at ease in their chosen environment. While I'm not suggesting every company should embrace 100 per cent remote work, I do insist on the profound importance of being yourself as a leader, whether at the office or working remotely. Many companies would rather focus on the 'doing'. And I certainly won't diminish the need to 'do' a great product. But the more powerful distinction, the one that will create greater sustainability and drive discretionary energy, is when you focus on who you *are*.

In May 2019, France signed into law the PACTE Act no. 2019-486 that stipulates that every company must have a lawful purpose. In essence, it legislates that a company's *raison d'être* (reason for being) must consider social and environmental principles alongside making money for shareholders. The irony here is that when executives in France responded to a 2019 survey conducted by the Institut Français d'Opinion Publique (IFOP) about what their *raison d'être* was, they answered that it was the company's *savoir faire*, which literally means: know how to *do*.[4] In short: to be is to do. But this is hardly a way to *be*. In a hint of the long road ahead for most companies, in this study, the second most popular term identified as the company's reason for being was simply *the customer*. There again, much like making money, having customers is not a purpose. It's a need that doesn't distinguish you from any other company. I ask: Where's the 'being' and how do the employees feel a deep, personal or enduring attachment when it's only about the customer? To wit, the challenge that Amazon will face in being limited to a purpose: 'To be the most customer-centric company on Earth.'

A strong North setting is all the more relevant when the winds and tide are constantly swirling around. Having a North Star becomes a lightning rod for corralling your energies. It helps to slash through the noise and take the tough decisions, including what you are not going to do. It will also help your performance in surprising ways, such as recruiting and retaining great talent. Moreover, it can also lead to improved financial performance. In the Havas Meaningful Brands® study 2019, it was reported that meaningful brands outperformed the broader STOXX 600 Index by 134 per cent over the latest 10-year cycle, had nearly triple the purchase intent from non-customers and had over double the repurchase intent.[5] In the same study, in a condemnation of the insignificance of many companies, respondents declared that they wouldn't care if 77 per cent of brands disappeared. Please don't wait for a calamity or a life-changing event to start your journey towards a more meaningful existence!

So, the gauntlet is laid down: Who are you and how do you want to be remembered?

Facilitating conflict

The four paradoxes below underpin our experience as human beings, much less as consumers and employees. I will elaborate on each of these four key paradoxes and demonstrate how and why we, as leaders, must accept them. Using the motto *Branding gets Personal*, leaders need to learn how to embrace the personal side of life, let flourish their personality and embed a culture where imperfection and showing vulnerability are acceptable. Leaders need to set the example for where the appropriate line of the company's culture sits. In that messiness, there are inevitably contradictions, tensions and conflicts. Not everyone can be happy. That's a challenge in an environment where political correctness tends to encourage sugar-coating of messages. But we need that asperity. It's one of the necessary inputs from accepting diversity into your executive committee. How are you going to manage those conflicting positions? We need to enable different positions, even unpopular ones, to flourish. The boss needs to accept that they can be challenged as well. Whether it's a culture of consensus, cynical silence or the HIPPO (highest paid person's opinion), you need to find ways to break down the walls and permit healthy debate. As Priya Parker, author of *The Art of Gathering*, said, 'Unhealthy peace can be as threatening to human connection as unhealthy conflict.'[6] We'd better accept that it's a messy world and embrace the duality, conflicts and paradoxes.

Managing energy and managing time

Before we get into the four key paradoxes, we need to address one more critical and often underexplored topic: our energy. Energy, like time, is a finite resource. The two are correlated in more ways than one. The more energetic you feel, the faster time will appear to pass. The less energy you need to expend, the more efficient you become. The more the activities you undertake energize you, the keener you will be to mobilize your time for them. It's about allocating your discretionary energy, alacrity, enthusiasm and generosity that will become a defining competitive advantage.

KEY INSIGHT

When you know *why* you are doing what you do, and it resonates with your deeper purpose, all the activities that are aligned with that purpose will bring you back energy.

From a strategic perspective, it makes sense to talk about time allocation. It's the scarcest resource out there and while it might be 'nice' to try to listen to everyone and patiently accept every different input, we do need to know how to decide and act. As such, a leader is essentially a conductor, keeping the rhythm of the score in play. You need to be not only master of your own schedule, you are a steward of your teammates' time. It's as strategic to manage as the money in the coffers. You should feel a sense of responsibility for everyone's time. Consequently, you need to show up and be on time yourself as much as is humanly possible. In today's fully connected global village, where meetings and conference calls are a very regular occurrence, the way you manage time bespeaks of your philosophy on life. This book is not about time management, but it's not possible to ignore how different and difficult it has become for executives, especially those who weren't brought up in the era of the internet, to adapt to the new pressures and speed of operation. It is with the additional pressure of time that the management of these paradoxes takes on all its importance.

Business cases: LEGO and L'Oréal

Never does one thing explain the lasting success of a company. Take LEGO. You wouldn't know it today considering its sprawling presence and success around the world, but it wasn't long ago that LEGO nearly went out of business. Privately held, the company registered huge losses around the turn of this century and racked up $800 million in debt.[7] It had gone from a company that played well (LEGO essentially means to 'play well' in Danish) to a company that had played too much. During the 1990s, it executed the classic mistake of innovation for innovation's sake. Despite seemingly trying to follow all the best techniques for spurring innovation, LEGO seemed to go after everything that moved. It had lost touch with its purpose. My belief is that it was a case of too many priorities. In 1985, Kjeld

Kirk Kristiansen, the owner and then-CEO, established the 11 paradoxes of leadership that he introduced into the management seminars.[8] This list of 11 items was symptomatic of the LEGO issue. It's not that its set of paradoxes was wrong or inappropriate. It's just there were too many. Aside from being too difficult for everyone to memorize 11 of anything, it's just not a strategic way to navigate a business.

L'Oréal on the other hand always presented one single and rather captivating paradox. It was François Dalle, CEO from 1957 to 1984, who cleverly created the image that, to work at L'Oréal, you had to be both peasant and poet to thrive. It certainly resonated with me. And it spoke to the need to be creative and to work hard, qualities which underlay pretty much all the top-flight managers.

Yes, we are filled with many contradictory forces, but the key to developing management principles today is to be strategic about how you expend your limited resources, and that includes how you plan to drive the culture of the organization. Furthermore, in today's environment, in order to be a great leader in charge of a sustainably strong brand, you need to ensure that how you operate internally is aligned with how you operate with your external stakeholders, including suppliers, distributors and customers.

Ella Miron-Spektor, PhD, INSEAD Associate Professor of Organizational Behaviour, wrote about the paradoxes of leadership:

> This mindset accepts tension between opposites, which results in flexibility under pressure and more creativity in the face of seemingly insoluble problems. Unlike classical thought about creativity, which mainly assumes the avoidance of criticism, the challenge of paradox theory is to keep shooting high, be passionate about your ideas, but also be able to criticize your own solutions. Managers with a paradox mindset are able to juxtapose different, seemingly opposing strategies.[9]

However, because of the challenge of sorting through the myriad choices, it's also important to keep your eye firmly fixed on what you're trying to achieve, and *why* it's important. In this manner, you will find yourself better able to make decisions quickly. Importantly, you'll also know what not to do or keep.

Paradox 1: We need to belong, yet be different

You're excited because you've been invited to a chic party where lots of cool people are going. You buy a special outfit and dress up to the nines. You arrive and walk into the room. Then you see it. You find someone else wearing exactly the same outfit. Drama. You belong. But, ouch, you're not different. The Bohemian in the Bobo (Bohemian–Bourgeois) trend that was all the rage at the turn of the 21st century in France was all about belonging to a 'misfit' group having a certain style, but also owning or wearing something exotic that made you stand out. As *The New York Times* described it, 'French Bobos design their lifestyles in a mix that includes the rarest luxuries, middle-class classics, senior citizen string-collecting strategies and student-style cheap-n-chic.'[10] The Bobos incarnated the paradox of needing to belong and also feel different.

There are two fundamental issues with the paradox of needing to belong yet be different. The first is that there's bound to be a risk of offending. The other side of belonging is excluding. When you decide you belong to some community or group, that means you don't belong to the other group. If you support Liverpool Football Club (as I do), then that means you do not support rivals Everton or Manchester City. By donning your club's official gear, you're establishing a border of sorts. By selecting the community or team to which you belong, you are differentiating yourself. In so doing, you enable an identity. There is no identity without differentiation. In a politically correct world where we are suggesting we should accept all people, we're asking everyone to *sublimate* their own identity in order to embrace all others. That's a tricky – not to say impossible – task, even if the intention is charming. It's not just OK; it's a necessary part of the human condition to push for developing a sense of belonging.

The second issue is that, once you have identified with a clan, standing out as an individual also comes with risks. You stand out too much or act in ways that are not aligned with the group's mores or standards, you may be thrown out. How, as a community, you manage that deviance is absolutely vital to the long-term health of the group. For, as much as you need to create bonds and unify, if you don't permit diversity of thought and expression, you will inevitably suffer over the long haul. As much as each community or country has its culture, I hold as a global human condition the need to belong and yet be different.

> If you don't permit diversity of thought and expression, you will inevitably suffer over the long haul.

I recall a conversation I once had with a French colleague – let's call him François – and how he was flabbergasted with how some people blindly submit to joining a sect. His repulsion was driven by the horror of uniformity and perceived conformity. François was aghast. Could the sect members not understand that they had been brainwashed? That they had lost their identity? Disregarding the improprieties associated with some notorious sects, I explained, on the contrary, how members of these tribes could feel fulfilment and a heightened sense of identity for being part of a community. As far as I was concerned, the key proviso was the vantage point the members had before joining the tribe.

If, as in Figure 3.3, an individual feels agency in his or her selection, it's a very different story than being forced into a group where you are not recognized as a singular person. I took, for example, the US suburban life, as portrayed in the film *Edward Scissorhands*. The film satirizes the cul-de-sac where

FIGURE 3.3 Agency: individuals seeking their tribe/community

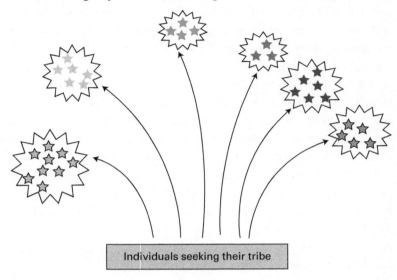

all households look like a replica of each other, replete with matching cars, dogs and post boxes. However, the point is that these individuals came to choose that neighbourhood because they were given the choice to be who they wanted to be in the first place. Of course, if you don't subscribe to free will, you might wish to undermine or reject any degree of agency and self-determination, but I believe in at least an element of free will. Even if we have genetic inheritance and cultural inculcation, the process of community building is what interests me. The people who join a like-minded community, who believe that they had a choice and feel that their individual identity was recognized at the outset, will more naturally submit to the 'sect' of a uniform suburban life.

Whereas a person who has been put in a box or on whom a system has been imposed at the outset (see Figure 3.4) who doesn't recognize individuality will more instinctively (and vehemently as in the case of François) reject the homogeneity of an

FIGURE 3.4   If individuals don't feel recognized, they flee

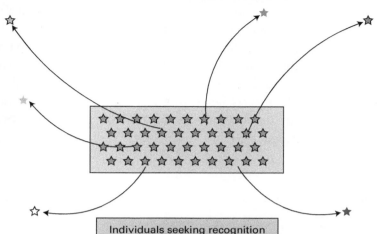

Edward Scissorhands cul-de-sac. For François, the cul-de-sac was exactly that: a road with no exit, a sort of prison. If you feel like your sense as an individual is satisfied *before* you choose the tribe, you will be all the more willing to join and accept the codes, language and rituals involved with being a member. The key point is that sense of agency that allows the individual to exist within a community. You choose to be part of a tribe, all the while feeling that you are singular.

At Redken, 'being part of it' was a key attribute for the team members, especially for the independent contractors (educators) that joined us. These hairdressers sought to join us to become Redken Performing Artists (RPAs) because they identified with our values and image, as well as the career trajectory. The candidates were carefully vetted for their attitude and willingness to adopt the Redken culture, its rituals, vocabulary and behaviours. Redken management was acutely alert to the importance of establishing belonging and ownership. Once an artist had demonstrated allegiance, he or she was free to bring his or her full personality to the game. The sense of belonging in Redken was modulated with a recognition of the individual. It was indeed a tribe, but the individuals who joined did so voluntarily and were encouraged to express their individuality.

Some systems and cultures force everyone to follow a path regardless of the person. Not only does the system ignore that the individual might have a specific talent and ego, it is a blanket approach that fails to recognize or give value to our differences. Whether societal pressure, an educational system or a business culture, this approach will not create an environment of fulfilled individuals.

Why tribes are important

At Redken, we all really felt as if we belonged to a tribe. It was a great feeling. I was happy to submit to the Redken way. And, within it, to find my mark. If you wish to create a tribe or lead a community, you must pay attention to the countervailing forces of wanting to belong but also needing to be recognized for one's difference. To tap into your team's discretionary energy means making each person feel that they are contributing meaningfully. Belonging to a winning team is rewarding in itself. It can be very meaningful to work with like-minded individuals on a challenging project, especially when you understand how the project is relevant to the overall strategy of the company. Sensing that what you do matters is key. It's reaffirming. It makes you feel that *you* matter. A CEO friend of mine talked about how his desire to show up (for his colleagues and stakeholders) was an enlivening sensation. He felt a sense of responsibility. As a leader, you need to model that behaviour from the top. By having that sense of accountability, where you demonstrate that showing up on time, delivering on what you promised and doing what you said you'll do, you are sharing your sense of responsibility. You're demonstrating that you value the other person's time. It shows that your word and image in *their* eyes are important to you. It's a signal of engagement and your humility.

Paradox 2: We need to understand our past, yet live for the future

It's curious to want to ponder our past, when so much of what we need or aspire to do is disrupt and futureproof ourselves. How much of our past should we worry about when we are planning for the future? Given the many quips and aphorisms, it's easy to be confused as to which one to believe:

> Do not dwell in the past, do not dream of the future, concentrate the mind on the present moment – Buddha[11]

> If we open a quarrel between past and present, we shall find that we have lost the future – Winston Churchill, 'The Finest Hour' speech made on 18 June 1940 in the House of Commons[12]

> We are made wise not by the recollection of our past, but by the responsibility for our future – George Bernard Shaw[13]

So, what's it to be? More past, less past, no past? Live in the present? Live for the future?

Let me to lay out the business case for why you need to understand your past in order better to live for the future. And the net of it will be to land you where you need to be. And the good news is that this train of reasoning, this path, serves everyone.

Allow me tell you a story. When I was running Redken Global, I felt I had the best job in the world. I was living the dream. At 36 years old, I was quite young to have been given this position. The then-CEO of L'Oréal USA certainly made that apparent to me when he took me aside shortly after the nomination and told me about the risk he had taken in pushing for my candidacy. As it was, in January 2000, I looked at my career at L'Oréal as successful, having had up until that point five positions in three countries over a seven-year time frame. In that span, I had married the love of my life, and we had welcomed our two children into our lives. I was an American living in New York as an ex-pat (go figure!). I was healthy, if 15 pounds overweight. I was travelling over 100 days a year internationally. Life was great. I joked about how I had gotten an MBA to become a hairdresser, selling shampoos that contained a special bond, hair colour that was about fusion and styling products that purposefully left your hair undone. It all seemed very special. I genuinely loved (and still do love) the people in the organization. And throughout my time as MD Worldwide, I was able to forge a strong and lasting relationship with Redken's founder, Paula. But it took a shock to the system to wake me up from a slumber. And my exhortation to you is not to have to wait for a similar life-changing wake-up call to act.

My 'moment' came with the events of 9/11, when looking out the window of my corner office in midtown Manhattan. I had a direct view on the World Trade Center towers. The events of that day unfurled in front of my eyes. I saw the first explosion and then watched the second plane fly all the way down, swerve right and around, into the southern tower. In the wake of those tragic events, I realized that it was important for me to do more than sell soaps and suds, as my great friend and mentor, Pat Parenty, who went on to be President of L'Oréal Professional Products Division (PPD) in the United States, called them. Pat would remind me, in his *terre-à-terre* manner, how our products were all good, much like those of the competition. What counted at Redken wasn't the product, even though it was certainly industry leading. It was the people and surround-sound service, mission and shared values that made Redken so different. As Pat would say, what counted more was keeping your word, being fair and delivering on-time execution.

In the wake of 9/11, it struck me that I really wanted to do something more. So, I turned my attention to the purpose of Redken: Earn a Better Living, Live a Better Life. And, as much as it was about creating success and being profitable (per the boss's injunction), I became more involved in the second part of the mission: Live a Better Life. If we could help hairdressers, who are so vital as the social glue in their communities, make a better living and live a better life, they'd be stronger and better able to serve their customers.

Creating congruency

If it were tricky enough to talk about a huge remuneration (ie earn a better living) as part of the L'Oréal Group, it was also rather inconceivable to talk about a better life when the reigning culture was more about hard work (I'd say it was much more peasant than poet, to cite Dalle's expression). Working alongside Pat, with the inestimable help of a visionary consultant, Howard Guttman, we looked at aligning the corpus of directors and above (about 100 individuals who formed the senior management of the company) around a shared strategic vision. At the same time, we sought for the employees to live the Redken mission. We wanted the employees to believe in and experience it. We convened together a strategy to achieve our ambition of becoming number one in the United States, and at the same time providing a way both to live a better life and to earn a better living. Our creative solution was to dispense extra free time as long as our company objectives were achieved, giving a whole new meaning to the saying that *time is money*. It was a moral and energizing pact. While this in itself doesn't explain all of Redken's success, it helped solidify the congruency of the brand and I'm proud to say that Redken today sits number one in the US market and is fast on the heels of the worldwide number one (that also happens to be owned by L'Oréal).

Connecting with your past

It was in experiencing 9/11 that I was finally able to openly embrace my own past. I had started a project 10 years previously, researching and chronicling the life of my grandfather, after whom I was named, who was killed at the age of 33 in January 1945 as a prisoner of war of the Japanese in World War

II. During those 10 years, I had managed to track down and meet 130 people who had known my grandparents, neither of whom I ever knew. In the process, I started to piece together their lives and came to understand myself more.

While I didn't follow the advice to undergo radical self-enquiry, as per the incitement of Jerry Colonna in his candid book *Reboot*, I did purposefully and methodically strive to understand myself better through the study of my family history.[14] I connected dots between my life and the tragically shortened lives of my grandparents. I started to understand better my father's life and to appreciate how lucky I was to live in these times, that are infused with marvellous new technologies and impressive improvements in healthcare and lifestyle. I then doubled down on making sure that what I did mattered, not just to me, but to my family and broader network. By knowing better my family's history, I became more focused on what counted and how to concentrate my resources. I became more attentive of creating a personal legacy. Making money played second fiddle to becoming a better person.

To be sure, it didn't happen overnight, but slowly I started to chop the wood and carry the water, as the Chinese proverb goes. I started to grow into the person I wanted to be. I got help from some key people along the way, including Clément Boyé, who helped me to write my first personal North direction statement:

To move people with grace to create meaningful plenitude.

By digging deeper into who I was, I was able to identify how and where my personal values and purpose overlapped with my career. And, by the time we moved back to Paris, I knew that it was time for me to carve another trajectory in my life. So, I left L'Oréal and started being more aligned between my personal and professional selves. I don't regret the journey I had along the way. On the contrary, I relish the souvenirs and learnings and many friends with whom I am still regularly in contact, especially those of the Redken era. They're all part of my story. When you have found a greater congruence between your personal and professional activities, you find a vivifying source of energy that carries through your entire day. That is the path that led me to where I am today.

> Never forget where you come from.

Make it personal

As business leaders, we have been trained to bring in the numbers. The messier 'soft' side of managing people is harder to teach; it's best learned through experience. Understanding emotions, empathy and ethics is a foundational element of good soft skills. As many might have it, though, the personal sphere is to be left at home. I disagree. By bringing your personal self to the office and by digging into your inner motivations, you will be better able to access a more positive energy within yourself. Inevitably, when I see how some managers mistreat their employees, not only do I feel sorry for the employees and think of the chips being left on the table, it signals some other type of issue, linked to a deeper fear. When you uncover yourself, you will do just that: you'll expose a version of yourself that is more raw, imperfect and vulnerable. And it's OK to not be OK all the time. It's the more authentic you and you'll be better for it, over the long term.[15] We all have weaknesses, that show up in being, for example, over-controlling, irascible or indecisive. Getting to the bottom of how you are will help unwind some of the weakness and allow you to be a more serene and better leader. I'm not clamouring for you to lie prostrate on a couch to reveal all your darkest secrets as Colonna invites, although under his stewardship, I'm sure the process is powerful; but at least you ought to check in with why you feel the need to be bitter or aggressive or downright nasty. In the next chapters, we'll explore in more detail how exactly I suggest you tackle this. But, for now, back to the business case.

Aligning with your brand

When you as a leader are aligned with the purpose and the values of the company for which you're working, the fluidity and energies at work are bound to be above average. When you consider that 7 out of 10 employees feel disengaged at work, this is a key starting point.[16] And when you know how to gain that alignment, you will create the biggest sustainable competitive edge: a team that is ready to deliver results together. So, in order for you and your HR department to be able to identify and hire the right talent, it's important to understand who you are as an organization. Your brand culture is necessarily a facet of the past. The way you do things, the style of communication, the language and rituals you have developed, are fashioned by your past behaviours. They may not be what you want or the best way to do things, but for now, they exist. If you want to operate differently, you need to be aware of where you come from. You need to have radical candour. The more honest you are with yourself, the more likely you will be able to transform. But self-awareness is difficult if you, as leader, aren't prepared to hear some criticism about yourself.

It's OK to not be OK all the time.

I know plenty of CEOs who say they'd like to be challenged and say that they embrace 360 degrees of appreciation; but in reality, their body language, not to mention their actions, betray a whole other truth. Whether you're running a start-up, a business unit in a multinational or the whole company itself, you are setting an example that is always going to be under a microscope. I recall how a member of my team would pick up on some of my mannerisms when I was listening to someone else speak. Each gesture was being read for signs of approval or disapproval. To use football terminology, even when you're not the person playing the ball, the work you do away from the ball is important, too. And, for the individuals concerned about your brand, your history can and should become a central part of your storytelling. Many start-ups feel that they don't have the time to spend on branding. Or perhaps they don't give enough value to branding. But, within your history, the original reason for your existence, the challenges you faced to survive, the partners and suppliers with whom you worked to get to where you got, are the sauciest ingredients to create your authentic and original brand story. They are genuine and unique. In a world of many me-toos, sticking out and standing for something are vital for your long-term success. As you look to craft your brand story and make it stand out, here are four ways to harness your past, present and future:

- Don't count on your past to make or save you.
- Your past serves to feed your future story.
- Make sure every day counts and contributes to your purpose.
- Because every day you operate will become the past and builds your future.

Sitting on your laurels or overvaluing your past is, however, poor form. Just because a company was 'established in 1907' is no prediction of success in the future. Companies that relish celebrating their 100th anniversary are relating neither to their customers nor to their employees, none of whom was around 100 years ago. Rather, I recommend injecting notions of where you come from into what you stand for, to reinforce the legitimacy of your purpose. In so doing, it should help inform what's important for you in the future and how to make the tough strategic decisions. Once you know who you are and what you stand for, it becomes so much easier to identify and say no to extraneous activities that, individually, might be justifiable, but don't fit into the bigger picture. By channelling that understanding of the past into the vision for the future, the true gift is that you can focus on the present, on delivering the employee and customer experiences day in and day out.

So, here's where we land. Once you have properly explored and shared a common understanding of your past, you'll be more aligned on the strategic direction for the future, and thus kick into turbo-power by being fully present and aware every day.

Paradox 3: We must reconcile the quest for order in the presence of chaos

René Descartes wrote in the *Discourse on Method*[17] about how the human being is programmed to decode and act on the reality that he or she observes. It's inscribed in our DNA to want to explore and understand everything around us. What is science if it's not the desire to grasp and quantify the world? I marvel at how mathematicians (and certain economists) are able to express virtually anything as a formula. With the progress being made in science, I believe it's fair to say that some are looking to master and, even, toy around with nature. In any event, thanks to some monumental breakthroughs and supported by new technologies, we are codifying the world and churning out vast reams of data at a dizzying pace. Almost anything real can now be converted into data. Lord Kelvin, the 19th-century British scientist, said, 'When you can measure what you are speaking about, and express it in numbers, you know something about it; but when you cannot measure it, when you cannot express it in numbers, your knowledge is of a meagre and unsatisfactory kind.'[18] Putting labels onto things and organizing the messiness are needs that are deeply ingrained in us to help make them real. We generalize because it's a way to perceive and learn about the world around us. We give each other names to be able to address one another. Governments ascribe us numbers. We codify molecules, plants, animals, stars, comets, planets and more. We love to put things into order, and it also helps us to understand our surroundings. But that doesn't work easily for all things human.

Messiness is, well, messy. Change is an instigator of disorder. The mind that seeks only order to work will struggle with change. These are the individuals who, when confronted by disorder, will feel the compulsion to categorize. It's the way they're wired. I spot them easily in the sessions I run when, as soon as they sit down, they will clean up the pre-prepared messiness that I assemble on their tables. The issue isn't just that change is messy. It's not even that learning how to deal with ongoing messiness is a mindset that is incredibly helpful in business today. It goes further than that. It's that chaos is a natural part of our lives. At a personal level, every person will face some chaos, whether it's because of the train that's delayed, a child that comes down with a cold, or a sudden change in weather. As you go on, everyone experiences unexpected misfortunes. These are not predictable events. These unexpected events are so regular, though, that you wonder how they aren't more anticipated. In a somewhat prosaic manner, chaos and capitalism's creative destruction are a stimulus for creativity. When I first read Brian Greene's *The Elegant Universe*[19] and discovered quantum physics, the concept of chaos triggered a deep level of fascination. The notion that a ball thrown repeatedly at a wall, subject to the chaos theory or quantum tunnelling, might one time pass right through the wall blows the mind. However, in a business world, where we need to craft plans, fill in lines in a P&L and produce to a schedule, it's normal to need to create order. Yet, with these new digital tools and technologies, we need to change playing fields and mindsets. As I've written previously, we need to operate in an AND world, where communications are coming at us all the time on different platforms at high velocity. Where the rules have yet to be written. And where we need to experiment and dirty our hands in trying out new stuff. Most of all, we need to find ways to change our own mindsets as well as those of our employees and, sometimes, other key stakeholders such as shareholders and board members.

It's a messy world dealing with the human component. Human interactions are naturally complex. We have to deal with emotions and things unspoken. We must listen to one another and flex our empathic muscle to gain perspective and explore diverse options. As much as you might want to find shortcuts or fix your human interactions with artificial intelligence, the true leader knows that the magic lies in human-to-human interactions. As I wrote in *Heartificial Empathy*,[20] if your desire is to delegate empathy to a machine, first you ought to evaluate what is your motivation for making the machine be more human. Is it possibly to compensate for your internal culture? Second, and more importantly, if you are not empathic yourself and you don't exhibit empathy in the daily throes of your business life, you'll give the wrong brief to the programmers (a population known to be less empathic) and you'll certainly fail to encode empathy into the machine.

You will need to embrace the messiness while seeking order.

Once you embrace chaos, you'll know that you need to expect the unexpected, accept failures, plan for contingencies and connect dots in ways that you can't predict. These are key components to the new mindset to deal with business transformation. Beyond transformation, it's about unlearning some old habits and deprogramming the need to put order on everything; and to realize that, in order to stay agile, chaos is going to be a feature of our ongoing lives. You will need to embrace the messiness while seeking order. This is a fundamental concept of a human-first organization.

Paradox 4: We seek truth but gravitate towards stories

We are complex. That's just a fact. We're confusing, conflicting and irrational at times and in ways that are mystifying, if not aggravating. As in the paradox of managing for order and accepting chaos, another combination that smacks of the same duality is our belief that we want the truth, yet are inherently swayed by stories, even those that we know are patently not true. Whereas truth feels secure, it is not a guarantee for gaining trust. In a world where mistrust remains particularly high of business executives (and marketers specifically), we'd like to believe that we're being truthful and therefore ought to be believable (in other words, trustworthy). But people don't hear in the same way that you speak. Everyone comes to the table with their 'truths' or stories. The average statistics regularly don't match up to the individual's specific experience. Just because you slap a fact on a presentation slide doesn't necessarily upgrade your trustometer. As research has shown, hard evidence that refutes your fast-held beliefs will typically fail to sway you or make you change your mind.

When two people attend exactly the same event, each person's experience and, therefore, truth is different. We may find reassurance in facts, but inherently we will have our own narrative. I have seen in myself how little facts alone will move me from my position. Furthermore, there's little more off-putting than when an individual starts the sentence by saying, 'To be honest…' or 'To tell you the truth…'. It feels like a precaution born of our constant fibbing. Stories on the other hand do have the power to move the dial.

So, what's it to be? I hear you asking: truth or stories? The key consideration here is that truth is far from an objective notion. Meanwhile, good stories, even when they are fictional, reveal truths about us and/or our society at large.

What does this mean for you as a leader: **you need to know your facts but deliver via stories.** This is easier said than done. The art of storytelling is not just in the arc of the story, but in the manner of the delivery. The objective of this book is not to cover how to do better storytelling, but I do have a few tips. For starters, I'd encourage you to read more fiction alongside your business books. This will have the added bonus of potentially helping you to flex your empathic muscle. You can also check out Neil Gaiman's MasterClass[21] or you can view a couple of inspiring TED Talks from Nancy Duarte and Andrew Stanton.[22,23]

The deeper challenge is being believable in the stories you narrate. An important ingredient to great storytelling – in the context of leadership – is the personal narrative. How does the story relate to you, personally? When you are seeking to gain trust, to build bonds and to inspire and motivate through your stories, you'll want to weave in personal elements. Not just of you as a hero, but of you as an imperfect and struggling individual, even showing vulnerability. **Truth and imperfection may seem like odd bed partners at work, but they also form a powerful cocktail for helping to drive a team to where you want to go.** It comes down to presenting yourself in a truthful manner. In an ever more transparent world, in any event, the more you try to mask over your imperfections, the bigger the liability will become. While truth, transparency and trust are vital to building a strong long-term relationship, storytelling is an art. As the old proverb says:

Never let the truth get in the way of a good story.

And from a brand perspective, as a leader, you will need to tell your brand story over and over again. Certain enlightened leaders, such as Steve Clayton at Microsoft or Louis Richardson at Syniti (previously of IBM), have described themselves as Chief Storytellers. As such they have embraced the role of communicating corporate stories that capture the hearts and minds. To the extent your brand story and life story can overlap will determine the nature and conviction of your leadership. In order to feel fulfilled as a leader, you'll need to delve into your personal side. You'll also want to explore your manners and methods when you don the professional hat. If you're going to work so many hours every week, you might as well be yourself at the office. As I like to say, with an intentional *double entendre*, life is work, too.

Recap of key messages and actionable points

- We're full of paradoxes and mastering those conflicting forces is key to the YOU LEAD philosophy.
- In terms of effects on your company culture, your leadership style and communications, the duality of digital and analogue needs integrating upstream into all your systems and throughout your processes.
- Transformation is not a destination and the journey will be ongoing, preparing us to use tools and devices that have yet to be invented and that will surely require more unlearning and developing new skills.
- When we need to juxtapose different concepts and our inherent paradoxes, it's not about pitting one against the other. It's about seeing how they can both live together. Part of the human condition is to live with our paradoxes.
- As much as you need to create bonds and unify, if you don't permit diversity of thought and expression, you will inevitably suffer over the long haul.
- It's OK to not be OK all the time.
- We will need to embrace the messiness while seeking order.
- Truth and imperfection may seem like odd bed partners at work, but they also form a powerful cocktail for helping drive a team to where you want to go.
- Life is work, too.

Endnotes

1. Fitzgerald, F Scott (1936) *The Crack-Up*, published in *Esquire Magazine*, February, www.esquire.com/lifestyle/a4310/the-crack-up/ (archived at https://perma.cc/XH6D-ZZUY)

2. Leadership survey conducted by the author online April–June 2020 with a total of 563 responses. Some 24.1 per cent declared themselves to know very clearly their North Star. While the combination of the top two answers (*know very clearly* and *have a good idea*) jumped to 58 per cent, the critical notion of having a North Star is to have a very clear definition. An interesting output of the survey, meanwhile, is that the respondents found it easier to gain full alignment with their North Star at work versus in their life overall.

3. In the same leadership survey, only 20.6 per cent of respondents stated that they were fully aligned with their North in their jobs.

4. www.slideshare.net/CabinetNoCom/no-com-le-baromtre-de-la-raison-dtre/ (archived at https://perma.cc/LKG6-D8HS) (slide #25)

5. www.meaningful-brands.com/en (archived at https://perma.cc/37YL-5YTG)

6. freakonomics.com/podcast/meetings/ (archived at https://perma.cc/5YWR-6WEJ)

7. www.imd.org/research-knowledge/for-educators/case-studies/the-lego-group-family-business-resilience-a/ (archived at https://perma.cc/E6NC-GT6X)

8. www.lego.com/en-us/lego-history/management-strategies-a662c1fd48894ad98 c81cee662c01744 (archived at https://perma.cc/LN6P-2FBB)

9. https://knowledge.insead.edu/leadership-organisations/embracing-the-paradoxes-of-leadership-12436 (archived at https://perma.cc/ZN4F-D7B3)

10. www.nytimes.com/2000/10/14/news/in-france-a-new-class-reinvents-the-good-life-bobo-style-has-it-both.html (archived at https://perma.cc/ED4N-WZ66)

11. *The Teaching of Buddha: The Buddhist Bible: A compendium of many scriptures translated from the Japanese* (1934) The Federation of All Young Buddhist Associations of Japan, verse 348

12. Copeland, L, Lamm, LW, McKenna, SJ (2003) *The World's Great Speeches*, p 440, Dover Publications

13. Shaw, G B (1922) Part IV: Tragedy of an Elderly Gentleman, Act I, *Back to Methuselah*

14. Colonna, J (2019) *Reboot: Leadership and the art of growing up*, HarperCollins

15. The Pratfall Effect is interesting in this context. As first reported in the 1966 paper 'The effect of a pratfall on increasing interpersonal attractiveness', published in *Psychonomic Science* by Aronson, Willerman and Floyd, to the extent you are perceived as being able, if you make a mistake, it will increase your interpersonal appeal, paperity.org/p/59814503/the-effect-of-a-pratfall-

on-increasing-interpersonal-attractiveness (archived at https://perma.cc/
L7FG-DJ29)

16. www.gallup.com/workplace/313313/historic-drop-employee-engagement-
follows-record-rise.aspx (archived at https://perma.cc/R5Z3-YNGL)

17. Descartes, R (1998) *Discourse on Method and the Meditations*, Penguin

18. Kelvin, Baron William Thompson (1883) Lecture on 'Electrical Units of
Measurement', 3 May, published in *Popular Lectures*, vol I, p 73

19. Greene, B (2010) *The Elegant Universe: Superstrings, Hidden Dimensions,
and the Quest for the Ultimate Theory*, 2nd edition, W.W. Norton &
Company

20. Dial, M (2018) *Heartificial Empathy: Putting heart into business and artificial
intelligence*, Digitalproof Press

21. www.masterclass.com/classes/neil-gaiman-teaches-the-art-of-storytelling
(archived at https://perma.cc/83PR-36AP)

22. www.ted.com/talks/nancy_duarte_the_secret_structure_of_great_talks
(archived at https://perma.cc/QHY6-T7VY)

23. www.ted.com/talks/andrew_stanton_the_clues_to_a_great_story (archived at
https://perma.cc/MMT6-S4FL)

PART TWO

Merging the personal with the professional

As reported in the Havas 2019 study, no one would mind if three-quarters of brands disappeared.[1] To avoid irrelevance or demise, you need to avoid falling prey to trying to be everything to all people. You will need to find agency and courage to push the frontiers, in spite of the risks of offending or disenfranchizing some.

Today's leader needs to be comfortable with uncertainty, regularly experimenting and on-boarding new technologies, all the while managing people and the business prerogatives. In an increasingly transparent world, leadership is under the microscope not just of the media and shareholders, but of current, former (sometimes disgruntled) and potential employees. One of the keys to sustained success is the ability to tap into the employee's *discretionary* energy. To do so, a leader must gain the employees' confidence and be prepared to operate as a whole person. This means accepting one's warts and all, and embracing uniqueness, imperfections and the unexpected at work. Authentic leadership means cultivating genuine connections with people, employees and customers alike. It also means finding a distinctive voice and not having to resort to committees to establish your convictions. Having a voice means you know what you stand for, and the more personal the conviction, the more convincing your voice becomes.

One of the typical characteristics of many entrepreneurial initiatives is that they were born of a personal problem or bugbear. I think of Audrey Sovignet, the entrepreneur who created IWheelShare, an app designed with her brother in mind to help people with disabilities get around Paris more easily, by crowd-sourcing the metro stops, sites and stores that were accessible. Another great origin story is from Emily Weiss, who founded Glossier, a unicorn-status beauty company. The reason for the creation of Glossier came because Weiss felt that there was a 'lack of personal narrative' in the beauty industry. She was tired of the beauty aristocracy (eg fashion editors and multinational cosmetic companies) being the only authority. She wanted to enable women to share their stories and beauty tips, no matter if they were a make-up artist or a 'regular' woman. In a *Financial Times* interview, Weiss said, 'I think… brands are increasingly like people. What are your values? What do you stand for? What are you speaking up on? What are you staying quiet on?… You have to stand up for what you believe today…'[2] In order for your company to do that, you as leader need to espouse those values. Sure, you personally may not be the founder, but you need self-truth to find out why you're working at the company; you need to understand where the cross-section of your values lies with those of the company. More than anything, you need to take your work personally.

Many large organizations are literally dying for that entrepreneurial spirit. If the new product pipeline is the heartbeat of future growth, entrepreneurial attitude brings the courage and determination to bring the innovation to life. Drawing from personal experience is useful in so many ways. It allows you to relate. It helps to imagine yourself in someone else's shoes. It provides a motor to push through the challenges and confounding 'it-can't-be-done' thoughts. On a very pragmatic level, being personal is effective in business and invigorating for innovation.

From an employee engagement angle, when a leader is genuinely personal and presents vulnerability, it becomes a magnet for attention and effort. From a customer angle, it's the space between the words on the paper. It's the recognition that I too exist not as a number, but as a messy, imperfect individual.

What you want is for your employees also to take it personally, to bring their full energy to work, to go the extra mile. That means they invest willingly in their work. And if that's something you genuinely wish to have happen in your organization, you'll need to model the behaviour yourself. Being personal includes having personal convictions. It also means being able to show you've got issues, all the way up to those of mental health. It won't always be pretty. Sometimes it may feel 'unprofessional', or worse, it may turn out badly and/or upset some people. But that's just it. You can't possibly seek to please people all the time. But, if the intention is honourable, you'll eventually win out.

> *To stand out, you need to stand for something.*

To stand out, you need to stand for something. The more that something is meaningful, personal and a force for good, the greater the chances that you will attract the types of talent you seek and create the culture you desire.

For all his well-publicized bad sides, Steve Jobs brought his entire self to work, obsessed by a need to create products to change our world and to enable us to think differently. In the hiatus when he was forced out of the company, he took with him a genuine culture. When the ex-Pepsi executive John Sculley took over as CEO of Apple in 1983, it almost killed the company. Then when Jobs came back in 1997, the Apple culture returned along with his irascible, control-freak obsession for extraordinary design, inspired by greatness with a purpose. His legacy lives on, couched inside his mission to make the world a better place. In his own words, Jobs wrote in 1980 that Apple existed, 'to make a contribution to the world by making tools for the mind that advance humankind'.[3] Not that I was ever a fan of his people skills or his being so outrightly rude, but in the company of such a grand purpose, many imperfections can be tolerated. However, I absolutely draw the line when ethics are corrupted, or when the atmosphere is corrosive. The challenge for a company, once the founder disappears, is for that mission to be lived front and centre in the face of shareholder pressures; hence the importance of the governance covered in Chapter 2.

In this next part, we'll explore the right leadership mindset, getting your company to be more customer-centric by first being focused on the employee.

Endnotes

1. www.vivendi.com/wp-content/uploads/2019/02/Meaningful-Brands-PR.pdf (archived at https://perma.cc/F4Y2-WN5Q)
2. www.ft.com/content/352ded56-b509-11e9-8cb2-799a3a8cf37b (archived at https://perma.cc/N2XB-ZSV9)
3. www.thebalancesmb.com/apple-mission-statement-4068547 (archived at https://perma.cc/Y9BY-5Q5F)

CHAPTER FOUR

CHECK

Your model of leadership

CHAPTER OVERVIEW

A precondition to be a great leader is the ability to develop self-awareness with honesty and courage. The new leader must embrace a new set of characteristics that are not generally taught in business schools, or practised by the majority of today's leaders. In the CHECK model, you'll find two qualities that are inherently internal, two that are more external facing. And the final one ties together the first four.

Sure, there are still successful organizations that are bred on a management style that is top-down and based on fear and control. It's true that some people would rather just be told what to do, punch in and out of work and get on with their lives. And, even in the most enlightened environments, there's a time and place for unilateral decision-making. Yet, I believe that a more evolved business leader must now adopt a different attitude for effective long-term results. I'd like to tell you a story concerning the Grateful Dead (aka the Dead) that I didn't think about when I was following them around, but that totally makes sense and, I'm sure, contributed to their success and longevity as a group.

Like many rock bands, at the beginning, there was a certain amount of fluidity as to which of the musicians was going to be a long-term fixture. Moreover, they had to change the name of the band as well once they realized that their original name, The Warlocks, was already taken. They then fell upon the Grateful Dead, which when you combine with Warlocks, can make them sound rather macabre. However, the true meaning of the band was to create a totally different type of music. One that stood out. It stood for something. And it certainly wasn't for everybody's taste. The six main musicians that eventually formed the core of the band were: Jerry Garcia (lead guitar and vocals), Bob Weir (rhythm guitar and vocals), Ron 'Pigpen' McKernan (keyboards, harmonica and vocals), Phil Lesh (bass guitar and vocals), Bill Kreutzmann (drummer) and Mickey Hart (drummer).

The Grateful Dead had a de facto leader in Jerry Garcia. For all intents and purposes, he was the driving force and the musical ear who vetted the talent. Importantly, though, he led from the centre. He didn't want to be the frontman as he was shy and introverted. But he gracefully fell into the role. Whether he liked it or not, he was the soul of the band. But here's the interesting part. All six musicians had a different musical pedigree and background. Garcia came into the Grateful Dead with a bluegrass background (he started out on the banjo); Weir's initial contribution was from early rock'n'roll (he was especially influenced by The Beatles); McKernan had a strong R&B heritage; Lesh came with a classical music background (he was trained initially on the violin and then the trumpet); Kreutzmann was interested in jazz; and finally, but by no means least, Hart played polyrhythmic and exotic percussion instruments. The mix of backgrounds meant that, as a band, they couldn't just assume each understood the other. To the extent that the band's live performances quickly morphed into long-form improvization, where each song could be 10 minutes or more, there was no laying down a singular backbeat where everyone would comfortably know what was intended. With their diverse backgrounds, the musicians had to listen and adjust to each other, accepting that no one had the anointed authority to dictate the order of play. As Phil Lesh said in an interview on Deadvids, 'That's how the Grateful Dead evolved as they did. It was because everybody listened really hard to each other. It's the only way to go. You had to listen.'[1]

The Dead, somewhat unwittingly perhaps, operated in a way that is suited to today's new environment with a form of marketing that inspired intrigue, cultivated community and delivered exceptional and unique experiences.[2] In this regard, they were truly ahead of their time. For example, whereas the music industry's business model was previously predicated on playing concerts to generate record/CD sales, the Dead made their money from concerts. Moreover, they accepted that their concerts would be recorded by the attendees and shared blithely afterwards. In today's terminology, we'd call that hot content in search of virality. It was obviously a messy route, but Jerry Garcia's leadership was always from within, in the middle. The band members were able to subsume their egos for the greater cause and to listen intently to one another. They also listened to and fed off the crowd's reaction. Once they had that framework, they experimented. They bounced off each other. And they opened themselves up to the resulting music. In another interview, Lesh said, 'What you can do is prepare yourself to be open; open for the pipeline to open and the magic to flow down through us. It means leaving yourself behind.'[3] And it also meant knowing that some nights they would be excellent and others absolutely awful. But the fans would accept this largely because they knew it was the price to be paid for making unique experiences every night. As we liked to say, when going to a Dead show, you didn't go to see a concert. You went to have an experience. The fans respected the band's intention, which was always about making an experience for the attendees. From 1965 to 1995, including a year off in 1975 due to Garcia's ill health and a few other band members' absences and deaths along the years, the Grateful Dead played a total of 2,317 concerts, which means they averaged 80 shows per year, each around five hours long. Never was one concert the same. In fact, no single song was ever played exactly the same way, and they had a repertoire of around 450 songs.

Check your mindset

The Dead were precursors in their 'style'. Moreover, in the way the band was run and how the 'sales and marketing' were done, they also employed methods that were way ahead of their time. Most of their techniques emerged over time rather than by design of some master plan. By bringing in-house the ticket distribution, they effectively made customer care their responsibility, not something that a record label or ticketing company (such as Ticketron or Ticketmaster) could ever do. In the early days, they instigated virality around each of their tours with a mechanism that was word-of-mouth to its core. They would not advertise ticket sales, but would announce in a discreet manner an address for an upcoming tour. Once a few core fans got wind of the news, the 'in' group would share it with their network, who would in turn share with their friends. The Dead knew that what they were 'selling' was a unique experience every night. They lived and breathed the CHECK mindset and definitely influenced my own leadership style. Each of the words in CHECK – Curiosity, Humility, Empathy, Courage and Karmic – you might have seen before, but allow me to explain with insights and examples how and why you will need to double down on your own CHECK mindset. First, a word of caution. Insofar as you might wish to pursue or portray the right mindset, unlike most other business traits, the mindsets we're going to talk about are not things you can just formulate, impose or learn. In fact, for several of these qualities, the very act of wanting to adopt them can be self-defeating. As Lao Tzu wrote, if you try to shine, you may dim your own light.[4] Similarly, if you want to be humble, empathic or karmic, you can't force it. It's something that others may detect.

KEY INSIGHT

The key to leading from the centre is to authentically own these CHECK properties: curiosity, humility, empathy, courage and karmic. The key to success with CHECK relies on your acute self-awareness and willingness to open up.

Curiosity

With so much change happening around us, there is an almost infinite number of things to learn about. It can be exhausting to try to stay up to date with every last technology, the new usages and dynamic start-ups cropping up everywhere. It's hard enough to stay current within one's own industry, much less what's occurring outside it. The issue with curiosity is that it can be an endless journey, with one link leading to another article that has inexorably more links. You can quickly find yourself diving down different rabbit holes, with a plethora of open tabs, saved links, PostIt notes and unread articles and books on the bedside table. If you're spending all your time being curious, when do you stop and get down to action? There are several important qualities that define the curious mind, fit for purpose in today's environment:

1 **Genuine self-awareness.** Only you are aware of what you don't know and what you should be learning. Do an honest

self-check about when you feel yourself bluffing about or overstating your knowledge. I would underline that self-awareness is an attitude that will be applied throughout the CHECK mindset.

2 **Unlearning.** You need to be prepared to unlearn some old habits and reflexes. Revisit your regular sources and assumptions and update what you're reading or watching on a systematic basis.

3 **Plan time for learning.** If you don't carve out slots for learning, it will inevitably fall off the plate, because time has a wicked way of being soaked up by whatever else comes around. Conversely, for the super curious, if you don't put limits on your time for 'learning', you will end up exhausting yourself.

4 **Experience counts – try new things.** Reading alone does not mean you know or understand what's going on. You need to try out technology in order to properly grasp the implications and what makes for a good user experience. For example, if you use an Apple iPhone, try out an Android. If you always use a certain browser (eg Chrome), spend a day on an alternative on Safari, Firefox or even Tor (for the 'dark web'). At a restaurant, look to order things on the menu that you've *never* had. In the morning, when getting dressed, change the routine when you slip on your trousers. We tend to always start with one leg. Stop and use the opposite leg. *Being* digital means *doing* digital and using the new tools, devices and platforms.

5 **Share.** Show what you have learned with others. It should not be top secret. Share with the world and especially with your team what you've found of interest. You can post interesting articles on LinkedIn or Twitter, for example. Don't mind that you might risk showing up your inadequacies or lack of knowledge. That's just part of the new learning experience. Permission granted: **No one can ever know everything.**

I have one 'curious' technique I'd like to share with you, which is to have a 'green' meeting every day. As I will elaborate in Chapter 8, a green meeting is with someone I don't know. Every day, I like to meet and get to know someone new. It's a great way to learn about new things and perspectives. Similarly, my weekly podcast, where I have interviewed nearly 400 guests, represents a great way to learn and pick up new insights.

If being curious is synonymous with bringing out the eternal child within us, we also need to get 'real' work done.

Humility

> *Who knows himself a braggart, let him fear this, for it will come to pass that every braggart shall be found an ass.*
> WILLIAM SHAKESPEARE, *ALL'S WELL THAT ENDS WELL*

If self-awareness is a precondition for continuous learning, it takes an even greater dose to develop one's sense of humility. For people who've enjoyed great success in the past, the task is deceptively difficult. As your success mounts, the people around you might stoke your sense of aggrandizement as they will tend to look up to you. Humility is one of the hardest traits to keep if life hasn't knocked you down enough. But why wait for that smack down? It's not your fault you don't know everything. In 2020, IDC (International Data Corporation) estimated that there will be 44 trillion gigabytes (or 44 zettabytes) of data in the world, rising to 175 zettabytes in 2025.[5] Just one zettabyte equals 10^{21}. According to a Global Entrepreneurship Monitor (GEM) report, there are more than 100 million start-ups being launched every year, which equates to slightly more than three per second.[6] With the number of machines, devices, nodes and sensors that are being linked to the internet, the number of connections is rising at meteoric rates. In this context, those who know how to make connections, to connect the dots, ideas and people, will be those who know how to surf on the wave of change that is ahead. I equate humility with letting go of your ego. Being humble isn't about being weak or an inability to take tough decisions. Being humble yet confident is another duality that can exist in comfortable harmony. Both traits can help inspire trust in others. Importantly, humility can help to connect with a wide range of people and thus to make more informed decisions. There's a growing body of writing and research about the power of humility. I highlight Martin Seligman, who described it as a positive force for higher-level functioning.[7] Insofar as it is still difficult to measure humility, one thing is for sure: when it's forced, we're quick to see the inauthenticity. And it's an attitude that requires regular tuning to make sure that any arrogance is kept in check.

As much as I would like to consider that I have a good level of humility, I recognize that with my profession as a speaker or, dare I say, a so-called expert, people want me to bring an authoritative point of view. Some people want me to provide answers to their self-doubting questions. It's easy to slip into the figure of the-person-who-knows-it-all. The obvious truth is that I cannot know it all, especially not for all individuals in their particular context. The answer inevitably lies within themselves. I like to believe that I bring humility through the delivery, in tone, posture and eyes. But it doesn't always work. I recall a few instances when my ego got the better part of me. In one heated exchange with an individual, I stopped listening to his opinion because I felt compelled to convince him of my point of view. I lost sight of what was important and felt I needed to 'win'. In another instance, I realized how humility is a quality that lies firmly in the eye of the beholder. When I was expatriated with L'Oréal from France to the United States in 1998, I remember feeling that certain people in the New York office

Those who know how to connect the dots, ideas and people will be those who know how to surf on the wave of change.

clearly didn't take a liking to me, from the get-go. I remember being stumped. What was I doing wrong? I thought I was listening and contributing in a healthy, cooperative manner, but it turned out that, despite being a US citizen, I was perceived as a foreigner, an implant from the French headquarters. The way they perceive you is *their* reality. I learned that I needed to double down on my humility, earn my place and garner their trust in order to overcome the belief that I had been sent to spy from HQ.

A sense of humility serves three important purposes to help you thrive in today's environment:

1 **Likeable when authentic.** Although the objective is not to please or be liked by everyone, being humble counts for those around you. It's a trait that suggests you are approachable. A humble leader admits to mistakes and, with self-awareness, seeks feedback to understand how to do better the next time. No matter your title, if you are genuinely humble in your approach, people will be more likely to want to speak up and lean in. In research released in 2019 by Egon Zehnder on organizational culture, they reported that Millennials listed humility as one of the top three most important traits in a leader (second only to strategy and ethics).[8]

2 **The better to learn.** As someone embarking on continuous learning, humility will allow you to be more open, to accept that others will be better than you in certain areas, and to listen without overshadowing incoming information. A humble leader knows how to take constructive criticism and thinks of feedback as an opportunity to grow.

3 **Collaborative spirit.** Humble leaders will give due credit to others. To the extent that you will never be able to have all the necessary expertise within your organization, it becomes critical to be able to collaborate without your organization. As a company, you need to find the best partners and outside sources, and that will require breaking down barriers to build rapport and establish trust. Every leader needs a team with

diverse skills and perspectives. A humble leader will recognize and appreciate the strengths of all others, in order to identify and create the best combination.

One of the keys of a collaborative spirit is developing mutual trust. I will never forget the rejection I received shortly after arriving in my new position as Managing Director of the L'Oréal Professional Products Division in Canada. It was a wake-up call and taught me a valuable lesson. As a member of the industry trade organization, I tried to persuade the general managers of all the major competitors to contribute their data to a confidential and big-name accountancy firm in order to establish industry market size and trends. Several of the competitors were not willing to hand over their data and the reason I was given was systematically the same: they didn't trust *me*. One competitive managing director admitted that he felt that I, as the head of the L'Oréal subsidiary, was bound to try to steal market share. I was stumped. Not only was our data subject to the same exposure, there was actually no way that I could use any such data to steal his business. The data was just to be used to establish market segments, trends and shares. Why did this happen? I figured out that, no matter my personal disposition and my attempts to establish a rapport with the general managers of our competitors, the reputation of L'Oréal preceded me. I had been doubly keen not to be flashy or show arrogance. But no amount of humility was going to be sufficient. The key lesson I learned was that perception exists in a context; I was being judged within the context of a longer history. Despite continued efforts, I was never able to persuade all the competitors to contribute. Despite honest intentions, you can't win every battle.

Building trust

Humility is a necessary attitude if you are open to leading from the middle à la Jerry Garcia. If you want to build a cohesive, high-performing team where everyone brings their full self to work, you will need to behave in a way that suggests that you are part of the team. It's a mindset that accepts you are at the service of your team. Some call this 'servant leadership'. This doesn't take away from the fact you hold the ultimate responsibility, but it's about allowing agency and tapping into everyone's discretionary energy. The story that I like to recount is the way we at Redken used to relate to suppliers and distributors. Historically, and still in many companies, suppliers (such as an ad agency, designers, delivery service) are there to serve us. We are their clients. And, sadly, many companies are keen to take advantage of prostrate suppliers. Similarly, distributors are sometimes considered a necessary evil, a limiting factor for getting product to market. In the fast-moving consumer goods sector, the relationship between mass brand and distributor is often adversarial. This comes from a history of mistrust and an unequal balance of power. At Redken, Pat Parenty opened my eyes to the idea that both suppliers and distributors should be considered as clients; in other words, the other way around. Only in this way may we end up with a relationship of mutual respect and become true partners. Some in the L'Oréal hierarchy, brought up in the adversarial manner, could not understand why the Redken distributor network was so powerful and effective. As the story goes, we liked them so much that L'Oréal ended up buying and bringing in-house the Redken distributor network.

In a study led by Dr Chiu from the University of South Australia, researchers correlated the quality of humility with team effectiveness and shared leadership, which in turn helps encourage reciprocity and shared influence among the team members. This was shown to have beneficial effects for achieving the team's objectives.[9] In another survey published in 2015 in the *Journal of Management*, data collected from 105 small to medium-sized firms in the computer software and hardware industry in the United States showed that CEO humility led to higher-performing leadership teams, better collaboration, sharing of information and joint decision-making.[10] With employee engagement one of the most important vectors through which to drive your business, adopting a genuinely humble leadership style is a proven way to help foster trust and team spirit.

Humility is not a sign of weakness

I hear you asking whether all people are capable of humility? You've probably seen enough arrogance around you to question if *all* people can become humbler? One thing is for sure, it's not all people who will do so. The key, though, is whether *you* are. Humility is 'not thinking less of ourselves, but thinking of ourselves less', Rick Warren wrote in *The Purpose-Driven Life*.[11] Furthermore, it's a quality that can be liberating, energizing and profoundly motivating for those serving with or for you. Within the minds of the more old-fashioned leaders, it's frowned on as a sign of weakness, someone who is timid, isn't confident or doesn't know what they want. I disagree. From a position of confidence and determination, being humble is the key to creating a sustainably motivated team and a secret sauce to creating trusted long-term partnerships. Humility is also a very useful characteristic in helping to find a path to purpose. With humility, you understand better your place in the organization and in this world. You are more aware of the greatness of the people and nature around you. **The real gift of humility is to accept that you are stronger for growing the people around you and for making the world a better place, rather than focusing on merely making yourself better off.**

Empathy

Empathy is a foundational attitude. It's a genuine superpower when exercised appropriately. Every one of us has the ability to be empathic. It's also a relative newcomer as a prescribed leadership quality. That's because, first, it's not a quality that prior generations of leaders and business schools have touted. Second, people are confused as to what empathy means. They often conflate empathy with emotions and weakness, and they think it's about being nice. Third, empathy is work. Just like being polite, empathy takes effort. Yet, the tangible benefits for increased empathy in business are manifold and provable.

It behoves me to start by providing a proper description of empathy, starting with the fact that's it not about being sympathetic, nice or compassionate. Empathy is about understanding the feelings, thoughts and experiences of someone else. We like to say that empathy is about walking in the other's shoes. If you're a man, while you probably can't actually find a pair of high heels to slip into, I'd encourage you to take a few moments to imagine what it could be like. The act of understanding someone else in their context is not easy. Aside from anything else – including how our ego and our own priorities cloud our reading – it takes time and energy. Academic research generally classifies empathy into two types: cognitive and affective. The latter entails the ability to feel the other person's feelings. If a friend feels sad, you too feel sad. Cognitive empathy on the other hand is about understanding – not feeling – the other person's feelings and thoughts. In my book, *Heartificial Empathy*, I explore this topic in depth. While I believe there is a place for and benefits in both forms of empathy in business, I tend to encourage first and foremost the development of cognitive empathy in the workplace. First, it's more accessible to more people. Second, it's immediately transferable from leadership style to design thinking to customer interactions. Parenthetically, it's also the only form of empathy you can legitimately consider encoding into a chatbot or other forms of artificial intelligence. Understanding how and why someone else is experiencing a certain feeling is a fundamental skill for designers. It's a valuable skill for crafting more engaging marketing messages. And it is a precondition for creating an ethical framework and for leading ethically. Most of all, empathy is a superpower for doping your team's engagement. As I wrote in *Heartificial Empathy*, 'The notion of an empathic brand – one that demonstrates empathy toward its customers – can only be durably and authentically crafted if the internal teams are legitimately empathic among themselves.'[12] Furthermore, there is proof that empathy is good for business results.

In a 2016 article published in the *Harvard Business Review* (HBR),[13] Belinda Parmar cited a study her team at The Empathy Business ran, showing that the 'top 10 companies in the Global Empathy Index 2015 increased in value more than twice as much as the bottom 10 and generated 50 per cent more earnings (defined by market capitalization)'. Included in the evaluation of empathy for the Index were categories such as ethics, leadership and company culture. In the executive summary of the annual *State of Workplace Empathy* study run by Businessolver (which specializes in employee benefits administration technology), they write: 'The long-term payoff of empathy, we've found, isn't just a happier employee or satisfied customer – it's a stronger, more engaged workforce and, ultimately, a healthier, more robust business.' In terms that are hard to ignore, the survey reports that '87 per cent of CEOs see a direct link between workplace empathy and business performance, productivity, [employee] retention and general business health'.[14] Furthermore, the study found that '96 per cent of employees surveyed believed it was important for their employers to demonstrate empathy. On the other hand, 92 per cent thought that empathy remains undervalued'.[15] Those measures are respectively four and seven percentage points higher than those for the prior year.

> *Empathy is a superpower for doping your team's engagement.*

While there are increasing signs that companies and business schools have awoken to the 'empathy gap' and the power of empathy to help drive the business, it's not an attitude that you can simply instigate with a magic wand. Like humility and curiosity, empathy isn't something you can enforce or teach. **As a leader, it's about developing your own skill, your desire and choice to practise such an attitude.** And when it comes to developing more empathy in your organization, it's about creating the environment for greater empathy. You can't truly dictate or teach it. You need to incite people to want to learn empathy. And that starts with you as the leader. You'll need to flex your empathic muscle on a daily basis. It's worth pointing out that certain profiles have difficulty in being empathic, including those who are well off and come from the upper echelons of society. Research conducted at the University of California, Berkeley, showed that individuals of higher social classes had greater difficulty than those from lower classes in reading emotions or showing interest in others.[16] If you're a leader from such stock and genuinely wish to become more empathic, you'll want to be sufficiently self-aware to take steps to compensate for what could be creating distance between you and the others. However, leaders often struggle at self-awareness. To wit, in the *Leadership Survey 2020* I created, 80 per cent of the respondents said that they had an above-average level of empathy. Yet, as described in the 2020 Businessolver *State of Workplace Empathy* study, employees continue to evaluate their companies as being far less empathic than the top management believe themselves to be.[17]

Just as curiosity and humility have important applications for your personal life, bringing more empathy into your home, with your friends and family, will also have positive effects. As has been noted in several surveys, for a variety of reasons, there has been a decrease of empathy registered in many parts of society. Empathy is a valuable skill, not just for being a better leader. It will also, eventually, provide a measurable return on your effort.

Courage

And I agree. My first book, *The Last Ring Home*, was a personal story about my grandfather, a US Navy officer who fought and died in World War II.[18] The book was subtitled *A POW's lasting legacy of courage, love and honor in WWII*. Through the dozens of interviews of World War II veterans I was fortunate enough to record, I came to a new understanding of what courage is. Courage is the ability to act despite your fears. A person who isn't in touch with his or her fears will inevitably suffer. On a battlefield this sense of bravado can have fatal consequences. In a business environment, it can have several unintended consequences, including, importantly, degraded people skills. As Peter Thiel wrote in *Zero to One*, courage is a quality that is even rarer than genius thinking.[19]

One of the keys to being courageous is to understand yourself profoundly and to register your deepest motivations. Deep introspection will allow you to catch yourself when you are behaving in ways that are counterproductive. For example, if you snap at someone, you may be able to find within your emotional reaction a personal issue that is entirely disconnected with the person or subject in question. Courage is having the self-awareness to recognize when you have hurt someone's feelings, admitting your responsibility and asking for forgiveness.

Courage is the ability to act despite your fears.

Wearing your colours

Arching back into my family heritage, I look at the courage that my great-grandfather, Senator Nathaniel Dial, showed during his lifetime. Although only a one-term senator, he was bold in speaking his mind and driving change. Upon making his last speech in office on the Senate floor in 1924, the *Philadelphia Inquirer* wrote:

Senator Dial of South Carolina told his Democratic colleagues a few plain and unvarnished truths... Here was a speech that was absolutely devoid of buncombe. It was the recital of truths which are familiar to nearly everybody except certain leaders of the Democratic Party.[20]

Without wishing to make a political statement here, my point is that Senator Dial was brave enough to say what had to be said. He felt that it was important to call out his own party, at the expense of his political career. On his last day as a senator, he addressed his old chieftain (Hampton): 'I'm ousted from the Senate, too, General, but we are both straight-out for democracy – and true to our colours.'[21] Even if the speech had to be retracted from the Congressional Record, he spoke his mind and the speech was reprinted many times for posterity's sake. His opinion was not partisan. It was for a greater good: democracy. I believe there are two important lessons in my ancestor's actions. First, know what colours you wish to fly. Second, be prepared to adopt them even if it will risk upsetting some. Of course, you must be judicious in your choices, but I do believe that the strongest leaders and brands will learn to have a more political voice as well.

I previously mentioned the personal branding efforts of Ronan Dunne, CEO at Verizon Consumer Group. He's got the courage to show his personal side – including his undaunted support of the Irish – in a public forum. Another stellar example is Alan Jope, the Scot at the head of Unilever plc since the beginning of 2019. In a publicly covered event he was speaking at, and in a sign of the times, Jope highlighted that all employees, regardless of race, gender, religion or sexuality, were welcome at Unilever. However, wearing his colours on his sleeves, as a Glasgow Rangers football club fan (which happens to be my preferred team in Scotland as well), he quipped, he didn't want 'too many Glasgow Celtic supporters'.[22] Obviously, this can offend some people, especially Celtic fans. Others may find it unnecessary or inappropriate. I choose to highlight the courage to carry your colours.

> Do you know what you stand for and do you have the courage to stand out for it as a leader in your organization?

My father, Victor Dial, worked for Ford Motor Company for 20 years (1961–81) and knew the Chairman, Henry Ford II. He spoke of Mr Ford in glowing terms with regard to his impressive leadership style. Here's how my father recounted one of several courageous acts he observed close up that were taken by Ford:

> Ford operated throughout the world either through its own local company, or through first-class independent distributors. This was especially true in the Middle East where Ford sales of cars and trucks were important and growing. There was a Ford office in Beirut, Lebanon, serving these distributors, including Israel. Israel was growing, and Ford had a good and active distributor, anxious to grow. In 1965 he negotiated a deal with the Israeli government for the local assembly of the Ford Escort. At about the same time, Chrysler agreed to provide kits for the local assembly of Jeeps, mainly for the Army. The two vehicles were assembled at a factory in Nazareth, owned and operated by the two distributors. The 'assembly' work was simple, the plant and labour force was small.
>
> In 1966, the Arab League decided to impose a boycott of companies doing business with Israel. Somehow Ford's name was linked to Chrysler's Jeep production in Nazareth. I'm certain the Beirut office tried hard to prevent it, but when the boycott was announced, Ford's name was on the list – Chrysler's was not. The Arab League demanded that Ford stop assembly in Israel, or else no Ford products could be imported to any Arab League member – virtually all the Middle East. At the time Ford was selling around 50,000 highly profitable cars and trucks per year to the Arabs, and only about 10,000 vehicles in Israel. For the Ford

finance department this was an easy call. The salespeople also. Stop assembling in Israel, return to just selling imported cars. The options were presented to Mr Ford. To everyone's astonishment, Mr Ford refused to yield. Ford was selling cars in Israel for peaceful purposes. There was no reason to boycott Ford.

The office in Beirut was moved to Cyprus. Our distributors in the Arab world suddenly became available to our competitors – notably the Japanese, who to this day have a strong if not dominant position in Arabia. It still rankles that Mr Ford's refusal to succumb to blackmail didn't receive the recognition it deserved. He was confident in his ability to make the right call.

I salute his bravery in taking a tough decision, especially in light of the negative financial consequences. I also like to encourage being courageous in the definition of your North and in crafting a bold strategy. If the strategy is clear, sharp and well shared throughout the organization, the handwringing needed to take difficult decisions falls off. The hard part is being sufficiently candid and self-aware to craft a precise North Star setting and to have the team be genuinely on board.

Courage in imperfection

The self-awareness of leaders is, however, hard to come by. Blinded by past successes and a title on a business card, leaders easily lose touch with their intrinsic motivations and can be misled in thinking how others perceive them. As a leader, it takes courage to acknowledge your weaknesses and imperfections. Frequently, when I see poor behaviour by a leader, it belies some kind of underlying fear, be it the fear of failure, too much intimacy or looking like a fool. Once you recognize these fears for what they are and let go of them, you will find it very liberating. For some, this can feel like jumping off a precipice into a void. On the contrary, there is something wonderful in understanding what you don't know and accepting that you will never learn as much as when you fail.

You need not be defined by your fears, nor by your thoughts. Having practised meditation every morning over the last several years, I've learned to observe my negative thoughts and to recognize more of my emotions. I know that I can still improve, but I like to look at them as clouds blowing in the wind. They too shall pass and dissipate into the horizon. I don't want to ignore them, but I don't want to become them either. I certainly don't want to be defined by them. **If you want to practise a new form of courage starting now, why not start your day with 10 minutes of meditation before you get on the fast-moving carpet of your busy day?** You will find a few recommended guided meditation services later on.

It's worth noting how courage is also a useful ally of humility. As Stephen Covey has said, courage and humility are the building blocks of integrity.[23] In the Egon Zehnder report noted above, the quality of courage in leadership was cited as the fourth most important trait. Employees aren't looking for you to roll over and just listen to the masses for a consensual decision. They will appreciate your ability to stand up for your beliefs to help sort out how to spend one's limited resources in order for the brand to stand out. As Jim Collins, author of the bestselling *Good to Great*,[24] said, it's about having humility and fierce resolve.

Karmic

The tricky thing about karma is that it is not something you intentionally want. You certainly can't order it, any more than you can command a wonderfully reposing night's sleep ahead of an important meeting. In the same manner that you can't tell someone who is stressed to relax or instruct them to have a genuine smile before taking a photo, you can't go about wanting to be karmic. This is the trickiness of the karmic quality. It's something that comes about. It's the magic that occurs when you've been leading with integrity, courage, humility and empathy.

The key word here is INTENTION. A lot of actions can be read in different ways, even polar opposite interpretations. An expression or word taken out of context may be interpreted differently than its original intention. It's important, however, to evaluate the intention behind the words and actions. Even if others cannot necessarily know what's in your head, you are the one who has a genuine understanding of your own aims. Some old school managers continue to believe that 'doing good' must derive a return. If you come at your marketing with such a transactional mindset, chances are you're basically more interested in doing good for yourself than for others. The karmic mindset is one of not having expectations. One of my personal credos is to give something valuable every day without expecting anything in return. To say that I'm a philanthropist or an idealist altruist would be far from the truth. But I genuinely believe that by providing and depositing value 'out there', it will eventually come back to benefit me somehow, somewhere, sometime. If not, so be it. There's no guarantee, but I'm prepared to take that bet.

I am not suggesting that companies convert themselves into charities or that executives turn into saints. This is a question of mindset. Let me play out an example of a brand demonstrating karma in action.

Business case: WestJet Airlines

It began in 2012 with a flash mob event that Canadian low-cost airline WestJet executives imagined and then employees helped perform for 166 surprised passengers on a red-eye flight from Calgary to Toronto.[25] It was conceived as a meaningful act and the result was a feelgood moment and quite a lot of buzz, including a healthy number of views of the video on YouTube (1.8 million at the time of writing). At the time, flash mobs were beginning to be a *thing*. Emboldened, WestJet management decided to up the ante and make a riskier idea come to life the following year.

They decided to perform a surprise on two flights in the run-up to Christmas 2013. The main idea, entitled 'The Christmas Miracle', went as follows: Santa Claus would ask every passenger at the departure gate before boarding what they wanted for Christmas and the WestJet team would then scurry around to have those very items come down the carousel in wrapping paper by the time the passengers landed. Can you imagine making the pitch for this proposal to the board? We'll give 250 passengers whatever they ask for. Worse, we'll need to mobilize 175 WestJet employees at three airports. How is one supposed to put a projected return on investment (ROI) in order to approve such an activity? The typical executive team would come up with all sorts of roadblocks and ask questions such as: How much will it all cost? What happens if everyone asks for an expensive car? What if... the present breaks or is the wrong size? Who's accountable? Is it legal? How many approvals will we need to get at the airports? How many customers might complain of not having been on one of those flights? In a blog post written on 9 December 2013, the stated goal was to achieve 200,000 views on their YouTube video, at which point a bonus would kick in: 'We're going to give Christmas flights to a family in need if our video hits 200,000 views. So share some Christmas spirit, help us unite a family for the holidays, and earn yourself a chance to win!'[26] Today, that video has been seen around 50 million times.

Fast forward to 2020 and the WestJet company has made a ritual of doing surprising activities around Christmas every year. The 2013 Christmas Miracle is the standout event and its halo effect is not just captured in the millions of views on YouTube. There is little doubt that the passengers involved still talk about the experience, especially around the Christmas holidays. And, more importantly, the positive impact on WestJet employees is surely the real ROI. The initial 175 employees, who had all volunteered, will also continue to be buzzing about how rewarding that experience was. Working at a low-cost, no-frills airline can't always be that much fun. But, at WestJet they have developed a way of standing out in a meaningful manner. As their marketing videos say:

It's better to give than to receive.

It's remarkable how profound that statement is. Too often, we forget its meaning. And it's not just because we worry about what we'll be getting back in terms of dollars and cents. During the Covid-19 pandemic in Spring 2020, we saw many people volunteer and contribute, based in large part on a need to feel useful. I know I always feel a slight dopamine kick when I can help out a lost tourist on the streets of London. But especially when the ego gets in the way, we often forget to ask others for help. It's one of the ways to insert meaningfulness into someone else's life. Allow someone else to feel needed. People get pleasure out of being useful. Moreover, if you do need a hand, you may be surprised how the help you receive may be truly beneficial to you.

KEY INSIGHT

People naturally appreciate the opportunity to help. It's part of the human condition.

As of today, the combined WestJet Christmas Miracle videos have over 60 million views. I am convinced that WestJet management consider the real return comes from making the slog of working for a low-cost airline a different and more meaningful experience for its staff. And it certainly makes WestJet look different to customers who get only a barebones flight on other low-cost airlines.

While some might be quick to suggest that WestJet's Christmas Miracle activities are just a marketing ploy, such cynicism omits the legitimate intention that the senior team has. They have proven that, without knowing how much an action will cost, they are prepared to put their money where their mouth is. Sure, it has come back to benefit them. But that's exactly the point of a karmic marketing attitude.

Karmic content

Other examples abound of having a karmic mindset and, although I can't get inside the head of all these examples, I single out how Ann Handley handles her work, as Chief Content Officer, at MarketingProfs. Ann gives away amazingly fresh, engaging and insightful content without asking for a handout at the end of each message. When you read her emails, you hear her voice and personality coming through. So, if you're running the customer relationship management for your brand, here's the karmic question I have for you:

> When you or your team pens your next marketing message, to what extent are you hoping for the customer to yell out at the top of their lungs upon reception of your communication: 'Hallelujah, I am so excited to receive your message. And I can't wait for the next one either'?

Until such time as you profoundly embrace that your customers and employees have a choice and that their time is also of great importance to them, you will struggle to develop a following that is voluntary, committed and powerful. Too many businesses that are, at once, selling to consumers and employing people, have lost the plot when it comes to gaining trust with their customers and staff, albeit for different reasons. Chip Conley in his book, *Peak*,[27] uses the term 'karmic capitalism' (that was first coined by Dr Bruce Goldberg),[28] and it seems that most businesses have opted to enforce a more transactional management that leaves the karma bank rather empty with both the consumer and the employee. As a leader, what acts of random kindness can you show today at the office or even in the streets to a stranger? You might just find it immensely rewarding on a personal level. As Alan Mulally, former CEO of Ford, said: [29]

> For the great individual achiever, it is all about me. For the great leader, it is all about them [the others].

The karmic leader looks with brutal honesty at the following three questions:

1 Do I know *why* I exist? To what extent is your why bigger than your immediate circle?
2 Do I trust myself? Do you keep your own promises to yourself? Do your actions echo your thoughts?
3 Do I like the way I *am* as a leader? Would your grandmother and daughter (fictional if need be) like how you are at work?

Recap of key messages and actionable points

An underlying principle of the CHECK mindset is that it is both internal and external. The combative and competitive spirit is combined with personal introspection and purpose. As you look to CHECK in more, you will see that one of the primary elements is your self-awareness. By being more self-aware you can properly evaluate and accept the areas about which you need to learn more. You can hold yourself accountable when you start to sound too haughty. You will set yourself more credible and achievable expectations. Self-awareness will allow you to explore more self-empathy and flex a more genuine empathic muscle. It's a precursor to being truly courageous. And, finally, when it comes to karma, you need to introspectively evaluate your intentions. The expression of those intentions will come out in how quickly or much you expect your 'gifts' to gain a payback. **By developing a habit of introspection, you will CHECK your mindset and find yourself on a more powerful and energizing leadership track.**

- No one can ever know everything.
- The real gift of humility is to accept that you are stronger for making the people around you better and for making the world a better place, rather than focusing on merely making yourself better off.
- Empathy is a superpower for doping your team's engagement.
- If you want to practise a new form of courage starting now, why not start your day with 10 minutes of meditation before you get on the fast-moving carpet of your busy day?
- Courage is the ability to act despite your fears.

Until such time as you profoundly embrace that your customers and employees have a choice and that their time is also of great importance to them, you will struggle to develop a following that is voluntary, committed and powerful.

Endnotes

1. *Long Strange Trip*, Amir Bar-Lev, dir. (Sikelia Productions, 2017) [film]
2. For further reading, I'd gladly invite you to read David Meerman Scott and Brian Halligan's book: *Marketing Lessons from the Grateful Dead*, www.davidmeermanscott.com/books/marketing-lessons-from-the-grateful-dead (archived at https://perma.cc/CJ2G-CJS6)
3. https://relix.com/articles/detail/dave-schools-interviews-phil-lesh-i-m-a-bass-player-but-what-are-you-relix/ (archived at https://perma.cc/XA7G-SCRP)
4. Tzu, L (1993) *Tao Te Ching*, p 31, Hackett Publishing Co, Inc
5. www.seagate.com/files/www-content/our-story/trends/files/idc-seagate-dataage-whitepaper.pdf (archived at https://perma.cc/V47B-P4JD)
6. www.gemconsortium.org/report (archived at https://perma.cc/N58H-874N)
7. Park, N, Peterson, C and Seligman, MEP (2004) Strengths of Character and Well-being: A closer look at hope and modesty, *Journal of Social and Clinical Psychology*
8. www.egonzehnder.com/leaders-and-daughters/explore-the-data (archived at https://perma.cc/BG4H-F3VL)
9. Chiu, C-Y, Owens, B and Tesluk, P (2016) Initiating and utilizing shared leadership in teams: The role of leader humility, team proactive personality, and team performance capability, *Journal of Applied Psychology*

10. journals.sagepub.com/doi/abs/10.1177/0149206315604187?mod=article_inline (archived at https://perma.cc/C458-R8BG)

11. Warren, R (2002) *The Purpose-Driven Life: What on Earth am I here for?* p 265, Zondervan

12. Dial, M (2018) *Heartificial Empathy: Putting heart into business and artificial intelligence*, p 57, Digitalproof Press

13. hbr.org/2016/12/the-most-and-least-empathetic-companies-2016 (archived at https://perma.cc/BE45-7QMM)

14. info.businessolver.com/empathy-2018-executive-summary (archived at https://perma.cc/HY7H-MCBE)

15. www.thebalancecareers.com/using-empathy-to-improve-your-workplace-4157504 (archived at https://perma.cc/F5XD-AGEV)

16. www.pnas.org/content/109/11/4086.short (archived at https://perma.cc/CS4G-99GM)

17. https://info.businessolver.com/empathy-2019-executive-summary#emp (archived at https://perma.cc/TJM6-BG7H)

18. Thiel, P (2014) *Zero to One*, p 5, Penguin Random House, UK

19. Dial, M (2016) *The Last Ring Home: A POW's legacy of courage, love and honor in WWII*, Myndset Press

20. Dial, R (1974) *True to His Colors, A Story of South Carolina's Senator Nathaniel Barksdale Dial*, p 196, Vantage Press

21. Dial, R (1974) *True to His Colors, A Story of South Carolina's Senator Nathaniel Barksdale Dial*, p 198, Vantage Press

22. www.pressreader.com/uk/evening-standard-west-end-final/20191003/282385516255333 (archived at https://perma.cc/G3UK-K2UQ)

23. Covey, SR (2012) *The Wisdom and Teachings of Stephen R. Covey*, p 52, Franklin Covey

24. Collins, J (2001) *Good To Great: Why Some Companies Make the Leap and Others Don't*, HarperBusiness

25. www.westjet.com/en-ca/about-us/christmas-miracle (archived at https://perma.cc/5RS4-UURA)

26. blog.westjet.com/westjet-christmas-miracle-video-real-time-giving/ (archived at https://perma.cc/V9SB-BGZ2)

27. Conley, C (2007) *Peak: How great companies get their mojo from Maslow*, John Wiley & Sons

28. Goldberg, B (2005) *Karmic Capitalism: A spiritual approach to financial independence*, PublishAmerica

29. The Art Of Magazine, Volume 19 (October 2019), https://issuu.com/theartof6/docs/the_art_of_magazine-volume_19_2018_ (archived at https://perma.cc/34QZ-AUJX)

CHAPTER FIVE

Employee-first customer-centricity

CHAPTER OVERVIEW

One of the key tenets of *You Lead* is the need to lead from within. When you know what you stand for, have the courage of your convictions and a brand that passes the Brand Tattoo test, you will be able to create a powerful culture inside-out. In this chapter, we'll look at how to create an environment where your team and employees are your most loyal fans and can help bring your brand's purpose to life.

Have you ever had a debate about whether your business should be 'customers first' or 'employees first'? I've yet to come across a businessperson who doesn't say that customers are important. After all, without clients you'll have no income. Some – especially marketers, designers or engineers – will clamour that without a product or service, you have no business in the first place, so you'd better be focused on creating a good offer. Are you nodding your head at all? It's a tidier gambit to focus on product functionality, price, shelf-space and ads than to deal with the messier qualities of employees and human relationships.

If human resources are almost duty-bound to say that employees are their company's number one resource, it's not because you say it, that it is believed or felt by the employees. I've seen companies brandish that they are a Great Place to Work, but intentionally close their eyes to the less rosy comments and issues posed on transparent employee sites such as Glassdoor or ChooseMyCompany.

Leading from within

While you can't ignore any of these business aspects, you also can't be everything to all people. The reality is borne out in the day-to-day actions. Of course, you want to have a great product, motivated employees, loyal customers *and* sizeable profits. But strategy dictates that priorities are established and allocated resources. At some level, however, the debate between being employee- or customer-first is uneven and often uncomfortable. There's a reason many companies shy away from being genuinely employee-first. The internal culture of a company is akin to a family. Human relationships are necessarily more intense and untidy. You, as leader, are living side-by-side with your team for an extended period every day. You are sharing experiences and creating a history. Depending on the sector, you and your company have interactions with your customers. As discussed in Chapter 2, if you're leading a digital transformation programme, you'll need to articulate your transformation around the customer as it is the most natural way to help organize what needs to change in order to create delighted clients. However, the more enlightened executives will understand that it is by having super-engaged employees that you can achieve

FIGURE 5.1   Leading from within and the Inside-Out model

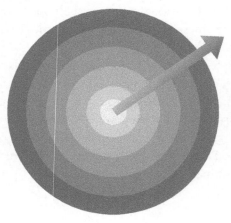

above-average customer delight. In this internet-infused world, with multiple channels, devices and touchpoints, the employees are the ones delivering the service. That's why the core concept for *You Lead* is to be *Employee-First, Customer-Centric*. Figure 5.1 represents the YOU LEAD philosophy. It has expression and relevance on two different levels: leading from within and being inside-out, employee-first.

The light and core energy radiate outwards. Just as Jerry Garcia did with the Grateful Dead, he led from inside. You are the light within, connecting dots, ideas and people. Think of yourself being in the middle of the madding crowd. On principle, you eat in the same canteen, you use the same facilities as the rest of the team, you listen intently and you connect. It's not because you hold the title of leader, but because you earn the respect. Your energy – with its imperfections – radiates throughout the organization.

The Inside-Out model

The second and related concept, as we'll be exploring more fully in this chapter, is called the Inside-Out model where the primary focus is on the employees. As brilliantly described by Vineet Nayar in his book *Employees First*,[1] the model holds that employees are the key stakeholders who make the magic happen with your partners, distributors and customers, and that by being employee-first, the rest will follow. Yet, to the extent that customer-centricity has become their strategic priority, most companies find it more comfortable to express their dedication to the customer versus the employee. An enlightened CEO friend of mine likes to say directly to his customers that his company is Employees First, Customers Last. It may take longer to explain, but it is a powerful statement that, at the very least, is uncommon and, more poignantly, will lead to a better customer experience.

KEY INSIGHT

What you promise to your customers ought – at some level – also to hold true for your employees. More emphatically, you want the employees to be the core embodiment from which radiates out the values, promises and service.

How you feel fulfilled at work should have a link with the satisfaction of the customer at a personal, human level. And when you're a human-first leader, it also must hold true for *you*, personally.

In the concentric circles going out, your role as leader is to figure out who are the key players and thus gauge the priorities and resources necessary to activate each layer. Even if there wasn't a formal expression of this model within Redken, this was how we operated (see Figure 5.2). The employees of Redken were at the core and were called *Redkenites*. This was just one of many special terms that we shared at Redken. The second inner circle was filled with the Redken Performing Artists or RPAs, who were independent contractors who carried the

FIGURE 5.2   Redken Inside-Out model

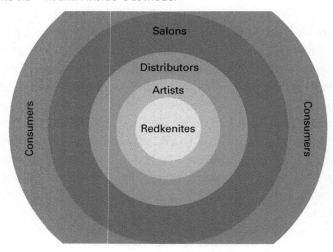

message of Redken, through educational activities, into the salons. Along with the employees, we were all part of the essential Redken Tribe. The next layer included the Redken distributors and agents, who were responsible for selling into the salons our products, services and education. Like the RPAs, this circle was filled with independent people and companies. None of them belonged to Redken. They had a choice and all of them were allowed – sometimes encouraged – to know and carry competitive products. Next, we had the salons and hair stylists and colourists, who were classified according to their loyalty and their Redken affinity. It is up to you as leader to articulate your Inside-Out model according to your brand and sector.

KEY INSIGHT

Those in the centre carry the core concentrate of your brand, in terms of culture, beliefs and values.

The partner mindset

The second concept, which I call the Partner Mindset, regards how you work with your partners and underpins an important attitude. Petco, the US-based pet food retailer, has undergone a significant transformation as it has converted from being just a standard retailer to a purpose-led organization articulated around the vision 'Healthier Pets. Happier People. Better World'. One of the standout elements of Petco is that they call their employees 'partners'.[2] They write on their website that they have 26,000 partners, which casts the relationship between corporation and workforce in an entirely different light

Your partners' success will lead to your success.

and, when followed up with specific and coherent actions, has helped to develop a powerful network. Help your team mates to shine and grow and you'll shine too. If you know how to garner your employees' trust and enthusiasm, you can develop healthy and voluntary employee advocacy, capable of aiding and seeding your messages in an authentic and organic manner.

If you genuinely wish to form a partnership with your employees, distributors, agents and third-party suppliers, you want *their* success. As shown in Figure 5.3, the key premise is that your partners' success will lead to your success. If you seek to help them grow, then you will grow with them. This can be explained with a mathematical equation, but it is more a question of attitude. Think of it as earning karmic points. Because you never know when you'll need a helping hand; but that point will inevitably come, and you will want to be top of mind and considered a top karmic creditor.

One of the major challenges is that people just don't trust companies and executives. That's typically true of the relationship between brands and distributors, which is a key issue for developing the partner mindset. As mentioned at the outset of this book, trust in business executives is low around the world.

FIGURE 5.3   Partner mindset

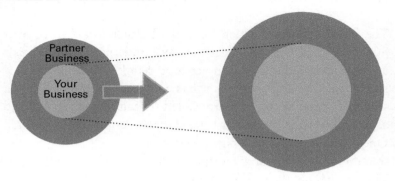

The Gallup poll shows that, in the United States, business executives and advertising practitioners (which I use as a proxy for
marketers) are barely more trusted than members of Congress,
car salespeople and lobbyists. In this context, as a means to
garnering greater trust, there's a need to prove yourself by holding your promises, doing what you say you'll do, and being
consistent and congruent across your stakeholders. One of the
great talents of a modern leader is the ability to operate with all
the stakeholders – managing all the differing inherent tensions
– in a reasoned manner. As was raised in the 2019 Business
Roundtable manifesto in redefining the purpose of a corporation, there are many more stakeholders than the shareholder on
whom you as a leader depend to make your business run successfully. It's not that any one leader forgot who the customer or the
employee is, it's just that our priorities have swung away, more
often than not in favour of the shareholder. Leaders who know
how to work with each stakeholder in a constructive and coherent way will be markedly ahead.

The Virgin brand is an example that stands out in the way it
has built its empire. Virgin is a loose confederation of some 400
businesses worldwide with varying organizational structures
and ownership models. Yet, it has a very strong and trusted
brand name. Despite the diversity of business segments, under

the helm and impulsion of Sir Richard Branson, Virgin stands out for its irreverent approach, no matter the seriousness of the industry. As Lucy Howard, Virgin's Head of Brand Strategy, described in an interview:

> It's the most paradoxical and unusual of brands; generalist and specialist, behemoth and start-up, deeply irreverent and yet highly trusted. There is no other brand like Virgin… [It] is also not 'perfect'; it's a human brand with vulnerabilities, which arguably contributes in great part to its appeal and relevance.[3]

And the magic of brand is that it spreads the Virgin ethos in the way each company approaches its customers, how it supports its staff as well as how it deals with its partners and the wider community. Knowingly, they are able to embrace their imperfection. Of course, at such a size, there are bound to be plenty of counter examples. No brand that big could ever be perfect. Yet, the attachment and trust in a brand are all the more believable when its imperfections are part of the narrative. Notably, Sir Richard Branson talks freely about his foibles, including his dyslexia. He even blogs about it, 'W is for Weakness', where he acknowledges his weakness and has found ways to use it to his advantage.[4]

What do you stand for?

Being Employee-First is about making your brand come alive by fielding a team with a shared mission, getting alignment across all functions and stakeholders, keeping the energies flowing and being in constant learning mode. This is no easy feat, but it can be done if you yourself are prepared to take on the mantle. One of the keys is to engage your workforce around a purpose and an answer to the following important question: What do you stand for?

There's no getting around it: to be powerful, this must be a personal question. You can't believe in something hypothetically or because it's what would appear to be the right thing to do. When you stand up for something, it has to resonate within you. Pretending or paying lip service is entirely counterproductive. A November 2019 study in France by the Institut Français d'Opinion Publique (IFOP) showed how employees won't be fooled by 'communications'. For the 500+ respondents, 7 out of 10 employees agreed that when a company talks about a *raison d'être* it's basically a communication ploy.[5] As I like to say, knowing what you stand for – your *raison d'être* – is about defining your essence.

In a world of plethoric choice and nudnik noise, you and your company need to find a way to stand out above the crowd. Unless you have a bottomless budget (with which some delusional start-ups thought they were graced), **the most effective and powerful way to stand out is to stand *for* something.** Without mincing words, you need to start the journey by being prepared to stand up for what you and your company believe. Sir Richard Branson is a great example as he incarnates what the Virgin brand stands for. Virgin's purpose is 'changing business for good' and it drives pretty much every decision. Even when Sir Richard goes on his adventures, it's fair to say that he's changed for good the image of being a stuffy CEO. But you don't need to be the founder or a raving adventurer to find your own path.

How do you lead?

As a leader, looking to establish what you stand for, there are three more prosaic ways to make this happen. First, here are three questions you can ask yourself:

- How would the world be worse off if your company didn't exist?
- How much of your day are you doing what matters?
- What political issue has significance to you and your stakeholders?

At the core of these questions are strategic issues of competitivity, employee engagement and longevity.

Loyalty to the core

With the Inside-Out model, the core principle is that your number one fans ought to be your employees, starting with yourself. When YOU LEAD, you are genuinely tied to the ethos and live the values of the company. You are the number one fan because you believe down to your soul in the brand's purpose, people and products. This is not an academic exercise. Too many 'smart' businesspeople believe that they can pull wool over the eyes of the others, rolling out what can only be sensed as pompous, if catchy, phrases and clichés, happy to carry a big title and take home a large pay cheque. They may be professional, even performant. But, at best they are playing a role and wearing a mask. At worst, they are treating their employees like kids. The real leader needs no mask

Your number one fans ought to be your employees, starting with yourself.

and considers the employees as responsible adults. When YOU LEAD, you're loyal to the core. But it's not because you say you're loyal that others will believe you. Loyalty isn't something you mandate. You'll need to act it and earn it, as I had to when I joined Redken. And many years later, although I left Redken nearly two decades ago, I can say that I count many of my old colleagues at Redken as bona fide friends today. I still refer to Redken as 'my' brand and continue to wear old Redken merchandise with pride.

We shared values and experiences and created a real sense of belonging that went beyond the walls of the corporation. Just as much as marketers are jacked up on creating Customer Experiences (CX), I believe that companies should pay at least as much effort on the Employee Experience (EX). How are new candidates identified, interviewed, recruited and on-boarded? What is their daily work environment? How are individuals recognized? What sense of ownership are they afforded? How are personal events – such as birthdays, weddings, births and deaths – managed? All along the employee journey, the onus is on you to find the best path for each employee, all the way up to how they might be fired or retired. What are the codes, rituals and habits that you will forge and in which you will participate to foster engagement and brighten the EX?

As part of our Redkenite culture, there was a code that said we were willing to accept one another as we were. As Pat Parenty described it, the Redken culture is inclusive. However, it's not just the fact that we embraced diversity or that we encouraged different types of personalities. It was that we encouraged each person to tell their story. As Parenty said, 'When you talk to salon professionals and you're open to hearing their story, their lives, you get a very different reaction.'

We accepted people exactly where they are and that feeling of belonging made them want to believe in the Scientific Approach to Hairdressing, Beauty through Science, Beauty with an Attitude and Science with a Sizzle.[6]

Ann Mincey, unofficial Director of Love, Redken

When you are loyal to the core, it's a professional *and* personal belief. There is a deep overlap between the brand values and your personal values. **To be congruent and authentic, it's about taking it personally.** And, as a coherent demand with immediate business benefits, at Redken we liked to follow the credo first set down by Paula's second husband, John Meehan, who implored us 'to treat Redken's money like it's your own'. It's a discrete dividend for any company when your employees save money because that's what they'd do with their own money. It's the very epitome of how entrepreneurs operate. It turned out that when

L'Oréal purchased Redken in 1993, something else became apparent: Redken employees were underpaid compared with L'Oréal (higher) wage standards. That was because at Redken it wasn't about the money. Once you are paid a respectable level, it never is. As my friend, Peter Mahoney, President of the Salon Resource Group, who spearheaded the Redken business training programme, always said, 'Treat your people well and they will take care of the business.' Many companies want an entrepreneurial spirit, but their culture won't allow it because they are focused on other corporate tangles and issues. Phillip Ullmann instilled a sense of ownership in his team with his own recipe: 'The culture that I like to promote [at Cordant] is a guilt culture: make a mistake, you are guilty; but you can repent, you can turn it around, you can change it.'[7]

Meanwhile, Ann Mincey taught me an important lesson about taking care of oneself, while working hard. She once said to me, without an ounce of guilt, 'Redken has gotten all I can give today.' Another way of saying this is that the work may never rest, but the workers must. When your intention is right, when you've paid your dues and shown your commitment, the leader is happy to retreat and spend time elsewhere because, surely, work isn't *everything*. You must learn to recharge as needed, to give yourself and others time. As Ullmann told me, 'I give people space so I've learned myself, and I've learned with my kids. They have to live their own lives and I give them space. And at work I do the same thing.' It's very much a congruent *modus vivendi* in your professional and personal spheres.

The Redken Hug

Talking of space, there is also the notion of physical space. The hug is a defining element in this regard. Among the many less traditional components to Redken was the Redken Hug and a specific handshake, much like you might have in a secret society. Both had a rhyme and reason but could appear to the outside like lunacy or sect-like. It could be considered 'too much', especially by those who prefer to keep work strictly professional. And that is perfectly fine with me. The fact that it repels some is as clear an indicator as any that you have a strong identity. It's not something that all brands can or would want to emulate as a best practice. Let me explain.

The Redken Hug was somewhat infamous, especially in L'Oréal circles. It made many of the L'Oréal executives uncomfortable, especially those in corporate human resources. For us Redkenites, initiated and led by our Director of Love, Ann Mincey, it became a standard that I wilfully embraced. One of our mantras was 'Redken Loves You'. And from the beginning, that mantra applied to staff first and *then* to our customers. A hug may not have been unique in the tactile hairdressing industry, but it was something that would happen inside the office among ourselves. Admittedly, when I was running Redken, at the corporate level I didn't go about hugging the L'Oréal executives. At the time, there weren't the same concerns around 'Me Too' as there are nowadays. Today, I would suggest a hug in the office would have to be done with proper intentions and express permission. But in the context of the 1990s, our Redken Hug was accepted, because it came with the right aims. I would add that, back in those days, I remember seeing people standing in the street doling out FREE HUGS to anyone who was interested. The Redken Hug was not a dogma, but it was a delightful karmic moment. Our hugs weren't the traditional tap-tap-tap hug, where chests barely touch. A Redken Hug was intentional, bonded and long. I liked to talk about it as the seven-second hug.[8] The length was a signature and it was longer than is usually comfortable. Why? Because we used to say that when two Redkenites meet and embrace, we hug until our heart-beats synchronize.

The benefits of a hug at work are legion and there's plenty of science behind the 'madness'. For example, a study published in 2003 showed that hugs will lower blood pressure and deflate increases in heart-rate when the individual is faced with a stressful event, such as public speaking.[9] Although the exact numbers are not backed by scientific evidence, psychotherapist Virginia Satir was known for saying: 'We need 4 hugs a day for survival. We need 8 hugs a day for maintenance. We need 12 hugs a day for growth.'[10] But there is plenty of evidence to show the effects in terms of reduction of the cortisol hormone (that is responsible for stress, high blood pressure and heart disease) and increases in oxytocin, known for promoting feelings of contentment, reducing stress and anxiety. The final, and most intriguing, component of the hug in a professional context is that the increased production of oxytocin also increases a sense of trust. And, as we've discussed before, trust is a rare asset in business.

We had our own language, rituals and gestures. It's not for nothing that we called ourselves the Redken Tribe.

Creating a meaningful community

As part of the Inside-Out model, each layer contributes to and can belong to the community. As part of the human condition, as discussed in the paradoxes of Chapter 3, we all strive to belong to one or other community. It's a survival technique as much as it is a way to gain positive reinforcement of one's own identity. The values of the brand ideally need to be consequential. For example, I think of *happy* as a rather lightweight concept for a company's culture. Many would like to believe they are a happy brand, but I consider it a non-position. When I first joined Redken, we were keen to promote the value of happiness. However, I always felt uncomfortable with it. To begin with, being constantly happy didn't seem right to me as an always-on *modus operandi*. As much as I'm an optimist and believe that I am happy because I smile, happiness exists in a context and is a temporary feeling. I prefer the notion of deeper fulfilment or contentment. You can only truly appreciate happiness when you know sadness. In terms of a sense of community, we did subscribe at Redken to the Power of Positive Thinking (PPT, which serendipitously happened to be the acronym of an ingredient in one of our star products, the CAT Treatment).

Accepting to belong to a community requires removing one's oversized ego. It means you are prepared to be part of something bigger. At Redken, we used the slogan 'Be Part of It'. In essence, *it* referred to the Redken Tribe. As the leader of the Redken brand, I felt bound to incarnate the brand values, to embrace the tribalism and not to shy away from those things and behaviours that made us different.

Building community on- and offline

Many marketers have latched on to the idea or hope of building a community online for their brand. If social media is now a given as part of the marketing budget, creating an engaged community on one or other social media pages is a dream for many frustrated marketers. Gone are the days of the 'free' community. You have to pay to play to get any form of traction online. Whether it's online advertising (targeted though it might be) or paid influencer programmes, you have to invest in order to gather a community online. In my experience with Redken and as a fan of the Grateful Dead, a commonality between them both is that **it is far easier to build an online community once you know how to do it in real life.** From a practical standpoint, each communion in a physical location is an opportunity to tout and sign up for the online space. But, more importantly, the skill-set and attitude needed to build events where people are prepared to get out of their workplace and come to your location are connected to what's necessary to build a vibrant online community. **The CHECK mindset is core to unlocking an online community and value.**

The Redken Symposium

In the case of Redken, we had a flagship event: the Redken International Symposium. By the time I came on board, Symposium gathered 10,000 people each time for a two-and-a-half-day extravaganza. Attendees included salon owners, stylists, distributors, agents and Redken employees from around the world. The event featured Broadway-level entertainment and the highest quality of education that Redken knew how to deliver, performed by a select group of Redken performing artists. Importantly, the stylists and salon owners paid to attend. They had to pay their way as well as for room and board. Furthermore, they had to forsake at least a day of earnings at their salon in addition. All in all, it was an expensive affair for the attendees. And yet, the vast majority of the attendees were returnees, having already attended Symposium before. The key notion was that this was a paid-for affair. Thus, the clients had full authority and permission to be demanding. Along the way, we wanted all those participating to feel valued and to enjoy being part of 'it'. Every attendee could choose their Symposium activities and educational course. Our intention was for every single participant to feel like Symposium was custom-made expressly for each person.

The brand you wear on your sleeve

As a further recognition of the community feeling, a lot of Redken merchandise was on offer. As a sign of belonging, salon personnel through to distributors and Redken employees alike were keen to get the latest Redken streetwear. At Symposium, back in my day, we used to sell one million dollars' worth of merchandise. I'm guessing that number has gone up since. Much like strong and meaningful brands such as Harley-Davidson, NASA, Guinness or the British royalty, none of which is known for its clothes, we sought to create sought-after items and apparel that carried significance well beyond the quality of the product. Unlike sports teams, school affiliations or music groups which naturally live off merchandising sales, it's far less common for a non-apparel brand to create such a market for branded merchandising. I (and my family) still wear my Redken gear with pride because I felt a deep-seated and personal attachment. If YOU LEAD, you'll want to find or mine that personal connection.

What would it take for you (and even your family) to don or collect items with your company's logo with deep-seated pride... even after you've left the firm?

The Brand Tattoo test

Going a step further, I have a test question I like to put to leaders who are keen to develop a powerful brand: **To what extent are you prepared to tattoo yourself with a signal or logo of the brand?**

For some, wearing the branded merchandise is tantamount to a *temporary* tattoo. Notwithstanding your opinion of tattoos, the question goes to the heart of true branding: how genuine is your affiliation to the brand? If you were to leave the company, to what extent would you feel foolish about having etched a logo on your body? How deep are your attachments to the underlying values of the brand? In Figure 5.4, 0 to 8 represent at best lukewarm answers. Only answers of 9 and 10 show that you pass the Brand Tattoo test.

If you aspire to create or lead a great brand, then it might be worth, as a minimum, figuring out what would make you and your team prepared to invest some part of their body with a figurative tattoo. This is a non-starter for people who are working in large conglomerates with many brands. In such organizations, individuals who will be moved from one brand to another and are more focused on their own careers will swear away from such tattoos. This Brand Tattoo test highlights the challenge in conglomerates of making a brand that is authentic

FIGURE 5.4   The Brand Tattoo test

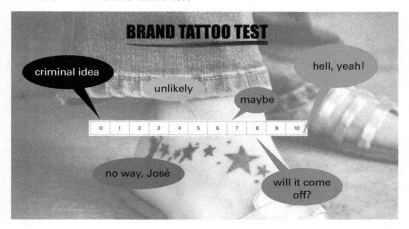

and stands apart. And if you're a big corporate selling loads of brands, how can employees tattoo themselves – even metaphorically – with the logo of a sub-brand without scuppering their long-term career aspirations? The key for you as leader is to find ways to *be* that brand, set the tone and carry the authentic message, such that others in your organization will be inspired to follow suit.

HOGS: The Harley-Davidson Owners Group®

The Harley-Davidson community is about as powerful and original as communities get. With over 1 million members worldwide, the Harley-Davidson Owners Group (HOGS) community brings together a wildly disparate group of people, from billionaires to Hells Angels to burned-out 50-year-olds looking for adventure. There are some 1,400 local chapters around the world. The communal feeling is naturally accompanied by Harley-Davidson merchandising and, in many cases, real tattoos. The patches emblazoned on the riders' jackets are strongly encouraged to help each member tell their story and their accomplishments. It's a perfect example of belonging and yet feeling different and distinguished.

Ben & Jerry's

Community at Ben & Jerry's is firmly planted in the DNA of the company and it all starts with the employees. Whereas most companies tend to latch on to philanthropic or social issues as part of a corporate social responsibility programme, Ben & Jerry's began life that way. There is a rigorous authenticity to their ethos that was inseminated into their culture from its inception by the founders, Ben Cohen and Jerry Greenfield. And, even though the company was bought by the large corporate Unilever, the brand continues to promote its activism and social justice causes through its activities and products (with ice creams such as *Save our Swirld*, *Americone Dream*, *Pecan Resist* and *Justice ReMix'd)*. Their activism is emblazoned on the website. Credit to Unilever in managing to leave Ben & Jerry's to its own devices (along with an external board of governors).

When the company began, founders Ben and Jerry presciently created a three-part mission that involved a combination of product, economics and social threads. Their first mission statement ended with the intention 'to make the world a better place'. While the statement has been tweaked, it *still* reads on the website that Ben & Jerry's social mission is 'to operate the company in a way that actively recognizes the central role that business plays in society by initiating innovative ways to improve the quality of life locally, nationally and internationally'.[11] And they put their money and resources where their mouth is, in tangible ways. During the Black Lives Matter movement, they were vocal and credible in speaking up, because it was a cause they'd espoused well prior to the 2016[12] and 2020 flare-ups. Along with the work done through their foundation, which continues to be supported by Unilever, albeit at levels according to the company's profitability, employees are encouraged to participate actively in community programmes. Being a leader at Ben & Jerry's necessarily means you personally believe in its causes and are prepared to engage in community activities, shoulder to shoulder with your team.

Question for YOU LEADers: What cause(s) would you be deeply proud of supporting and talking about to your grandmother?

Avoiding nonsensical causes

Not all companies were born with social cause and community so deeply entrenched in their roots. If you are leading a company and want to espouse a cause, the retrofit can be awkward, not to say misplaced. If return on investment or PR coverage are the motivations, it's clear that the intention is in the wrong place. It's a tricky line to tread between having a relevant cause that resonates

Your intention counts immeasurably.

with your core stakeholders and steering clear of striving for too blatant a payback. Furthermore, pragmatically speaking, you'll want to carve out a territory that makes the cause relevant and ownable.

I've seen examples of companies supporting a charity run for a cause that was more convenient than purposeful. On one occasion, I worked with an organization whose chief executive was proud to declare that the company would donate a percentage of profits from a certain campaign, knowing full well that the activity would make no profits at all. In another instance, I witnessed an agency propose an influencer outreach programme based on the ability to 'pull the heartstrings' of the influencers. It's important to recognize that your intention counts immeasurably. Not only will you want to evaluate your own integrity and intentionality with regard to the way you plan to make the world a better place, you'll want to see how recruitment and ongoing evaluations can be appropriately gauged and linked to the core mission of the company.

Crafting uniqueness

One of my obsessions when running Redken was making sure that everything possible had a specific and ideally unique Redken feel to it. This began with many intangible elements of culture and involved rituals, language, symbols and behaviour such as the Redken Hug. With my tremendous partner in charge of Redken Education, Christine Schuster, we made sure that the Redken literature for education was entirely in line with the look and feel of Redken's marketing and commercial messages. This may seem anecdotal, but it was important for us because at Redken we put education on an equal footing with marketing and sales, a pioneering approach in the industry. And it was really about having all components of Redken contribute to our identity. I would liken this to Apple's attention to painting the back side of the fence, as Walter Isaacson described it in his biography of Steve Jobs.[13] Apple designers would insist on elegance in the electronic circuitry even under the hood, where no ordinary consumer will ever cast an eye.

In terms of packaging, whereas we were pressured to synergize with L'Oréal's other brands to take advantage of favourable costs and factory efficiencies, we devised a unique packaging for our landmark Redken haircare line, code-named *Skyscraper* to indicate our unique attachment to New York City. The bottle, which is asymmetrical, ribbed on either side and with a mixture of geometry and rounded surfaces, was inspired by several skyscraper buildings, including the Met Life building that straddles Park Avenue at 45th Street. In this manner, an assortment of Redken haircare bottles can literally look like the skyline of New York on the shelf. As a leader, you'll want to pay attention to the unique expressions of your brand throughout the value chain, as shown in Figure 5.5.

On the right-hand side of Figure 5.5 are the more traditional elements of branding and positioning. On the left-hand side, you

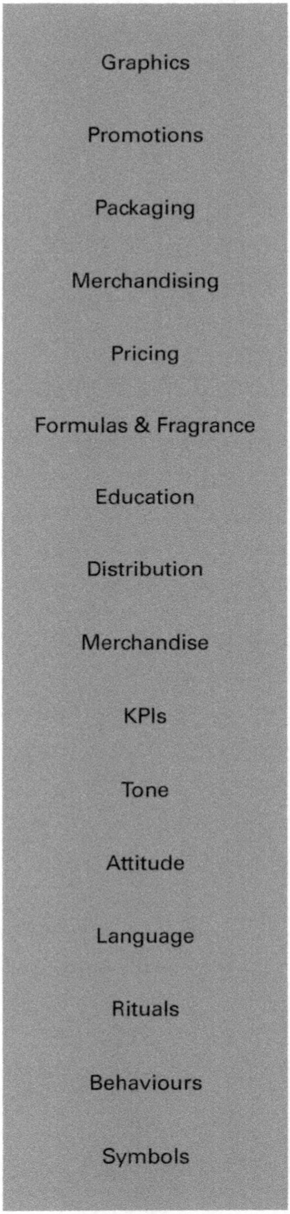

FIGURE 5.5   Branding along the chain of value

Graphics

Promotions

Packaging

Merchandising

Pricing

Formulas & Fragrance

Education

Distribution

Merchandise

KPIs

Tone

Attitude

Language

Rituals

Behaviours

Symbols

will see how the human factor is involved in branding. Some of the activities and brand activations are internally oriented. Others deal specifically with how to interact with certain stakeholders. The key as a leader is to ensure the greatest amount of coherence and congruency along the entire chain. It is trickier and messier to manage when it comes to people. But it's key to being an employee-first, customer-centric brand. It's the core concept of a human-first organization. When YOU LEAD, the way you lead and the people you employ are essential to crafting a uniqueness to your brand.

Making your communication congruent and consistent

One of the more intriguing reasons why you ought to be employee-first is that employees are the only stakeholders that have a front-row seat looking at the full spectrum of messages being communicated externally (see Figure 5.6). I classify communication into three groups:

1 corporate – towards shareholders, third-party stakeholders and governmental offices;
2 commercial – towards the existing and potential customers;
3 employer – towards current and future employees.

FIGURE 5.6   Employee-first communications

Whereas in the past, there was an ability to mask these three different populations, virtually everything is now exposed on the internet. Gone are the days when a CEO could talk freely behind closed doors about 'cutting headcount' and reducing costs to shareholders all the while promoting the company as a great place to work with its exhausted, short-handed employees. Similarly, leaders need to up their ethical game to be vigilant about aligning their marketing promises with reality. First, it's a more cogent and coherent way to operate. Second, with so many touchpoints and interactions with different staff, the chances of keeping unethical practices hidden are much slimmer. This new reality reinforces the need to be employee-first. It not only makes sense because the employees are delivering the customer experience, they will be all the more partisan and motivated if they feel that they are working for a company with a matching degree of integrity. The good news is that you won't be expected to be perfect in execution so long as your intentions are bona fide.

How to make purpose come alive – imperfectly

There are corporate walls on which missions and purposes are written where so many passers-by wince or roll their eyes. To be clear, in large organizations, no matter the very best of intentions, you'll always find naysayers and eye-rollers. That's true even at a Patagonia, Harley-Davidson or Ben & Jerry's. Creating a mission statement is one thing. Keeping it alive and meaningful is another. Companies go through changes in management, swings and fortunes of the stock market and unforeseen circumstances, not to mention straight-out errors in judgement. Nobody is perfect. One should never even strive for perfection. Such a target is not only unrealistic, it is debilitating. I liken a mission to a relationship. A brand has a relationship with its mission. There may be offshoots (eg family members) that are more or less tied into the core purpose. There will be times when the mission is more intensely expressed, such as at a family reunion or festive occasion. But, like any good and long-lasting marriage, it takes effort, compromise and a shared vision of the future. Your role as a leader is to help set the tone, show the willingness to remove your ego and participate in making the vision come alive. The more the purpose is internalized and feels right, you'll know more instinctively what is on track and what isn't. If it's an intellectual exercise, encumbered by red tape, ethical worries and discussions of return on investment, the chances are that you'll only provoke more eye-rolling. The ambition of a purpose is stronger when it is smaller and truer than big and unbelievable. You're better off aiming for one that resonates than shooting for the stars and trying to be too noble. For example, take the Chobani mission: 'To bring high-quality yogurt to more people and create positive change in our country's food culture.'[14] I like this mission because it is entirely consistent with its core business and yet is meaningful at a higher level and to a wider audience than just its yogurt-eating customers. And when its founder, Hamdi Ulukaya, speaks, he does so with humility, gratefulness and authenticity. It makes for a compelling story.

There are two keys to making your purpose come alive:

- Make sure your mission resonates from the inside out.
- Strive to do better for others, beyond your immediate circle of stakeholders.

Virgin approaches this by looking to answer a simple question: 'What role and meaning will you have in people's lives?' It's a profoundly important question that deserves to be asked.

Recap of key messages and actionable points

- What you promise to your customers ought – at some level – also to hold true for your employees. You want the employees to be the core embodiment from which radiates out the values, promises and service.

- Those in the centre carry the core concentrate of your brand, in terms of culture, beliefs and values.
- Your partners' success will lead to your success.
- Being Employee-First is about making your brand come alive by fielding a team with a shared mission, getting alignment across all functions and stakeholders, keeping the energies flowing and being in constant learning mode.
- The most effective and powerful way to stand out is to stand for something.
- To be congruent and authentic, it's about taking it personally.
- With the Inside-Out model, the core principle is that your number one fans ought to be your employees, starting with yourself.
- It is far easier to build an online community once you know how to do it in real life.
- The CHECK mindset is core to unlocking an online community and value.
- To what extent are you prepared to tattoo yourself with a signal or logo of the brand?
- Your intention counts immeasurably.
- There's no point in telling your staff to behave one way towards the external customer, but treating them in an inconsistent and different manner internally.

Endnotes

1. Nayar, V (2010) *Employees First, Customers Second: Turning conventional management upside down*, Harvard Business Press
2. Starbucks also calls its employees partners.
3. https://web.archive.org/web/20180306075613/https://www.virgin.com/entrepreneur/how-does-brand-virgin-remain-relevant-after-so-many-years (archived at https://perma.cc/DF6C-YVH3)
4. https://web.archive.org/web/20180306081130/https://www.virgin.com/richard-branson/w-weakness (archived at https://perma.cc/63VZ-V3VP)
5. www.slideshare.net/CabinetNoCom/no-com-le-baromtre-de-la-raison-dtre (archived at https://perma.cc/8FF9-CXBJ)

6. Exclusive interview with Ann Mincey.

7. Exclusive interview with Phillip Ullmann.

8. Research is not conclusive on how long the hug has to be in order to get the benefits. One study, published in *Comprehensive Psychology* and led by Dr Jan Astrom, entitled 'Meaning of hugging: from greeting behavior to touching implication' (2012, vol 1, Article 13, ISSN 2165-2228), worked on the premise of 10-second hugs. Another study published in *Behavioural Medicine* in 2003 by a team led by Karen M Grewen, PhD, entitled 'Warm Partner Contact is Related to Lower Cardiovascular Reactivity', looked at the effects of a 20-second hug, www.ncbi.nlm.nih.gov/pubmed/15206831 (archived at https://perma.cc/7HWP-NQ7D)

9. Karen M Grewen, PhD, Warm Partner Contact is Related to Lower Cardiovascular Reactivity, www.ncbi.nlm.nih.gov/pubmed/15206831 (archived at https://perma.cc/7HWP-NQ7D)

10. us.sagepub.com/sites/default/files/upm-binaries/53279_ch_6.pdf (archived at https://perma.cc/CP6K-XPC9)

11. www.benjerry.com/values (archived at https://perma.cc/5VW6-8QQT)

12. A message published on 6 October 2016 on the website: www.benjerry.com/whats-new/2016/why-black-lives-matter (archived at https://perma.cc/HMD6-V6PD)

13. Isaacson, W (2011) *Steve Jobs*, Simon & Schuster

14. www.chobani.com/about/ (archived at https://perma.cc/S5SP-HN7N)

CHAPTER SIX

Making customer-centricity come alive

CHAPTER OVERVIEW

Once you have established the importance of an employee-first culture, the next step is to galvanize all your efforts around creating exceptional products and services for your customers. Knowing that what you say and do for your customers must relate back to the culture of your company, you need an unflinching resolve to create a culture to deliver the best customer experience. Aligning the organization around the customer, using the appropriate digital tools, platforms and data; you have the opportunity to enact transformational leadership and drive enduring success.

The most insightful point about striving to be customer-centric is that **the very act of focusing on the customer is the most effective way to bring about transformation in your organization.** Let me express it differently. We're now in a digitally infused world where the balance of power has shifted away from corporate one-way messaging towards the connected consumer and where employees play a vital role in delivering the customer experience. Communications have become more complex because of the number of different individuals involved in handling the different touchpoints and channels, mixed in with evermore automated processes. It is by focusing on the customer journey that you will be better able to create a company-wide project, and that will help to prioritize your actions and investments, re-galvanize latent lethargy and break down internal silos. As we'll explore in this chapter, **the challenge of being customer-centric is that it is not an objective but a mindset.** Moreover, being customer-centric is no more a strategy than wishing to make money. And to make matters worse, it's difficult to measure and any benchmarks are constantly evolving.

As we dig further into customer-centricity, I stress that the real route to sustained success lies in making a genuinely employee-first culture and company. Employee-first is still a more uncommon position than customer-centricity, but the scientific evidence is growing to support the importance of the employee in delivering a superior customer experience, not to forget a stronger financial performance. **Considering the human involvement throughout a mixture of off- and online channels all along the customer journey, when YOU LEAD, you will want to embrace, enhance and elevate the employee experience at each stage.** And the key component for helping to make your strategic choices is to articulate this around what I call your *essence* or your North Star. More on that in the following chapter. Figure 6.1 shows to what extent human interaction from different parts of the organization (including third parties) will be involved in the customer journey.

The five points of the star in Figure 6.1 show five types of departments that, depending on how you're set up, will involve some kind of direct interaction with customers through employees. Some companies will have outsourced their customer service. Most will outsource their delivery logistics. Others yet will also

FIGURE 6.1   The human factor in the customer journey

outsource their retail via wholesalers. All the same, around each pole, your responsibility is to make sure that the relevant individuals – in seamless coordination with the automated technologies – create an experience for the customer that is optimal, and at the very least removes as much agony, heartache and irritation as possible. Each customer will have a specific context and typically interact with a variety of different individuals from differing parts of the organization. When YOU LEAD, you will be looking to craft a meaningful journey for the employee, such that they are appropriately equipped and know their scope and role in delivering the delightful experience for the customer.

Relating customer-centricity to the customer experience

The quest for customer-centricity is a journey, not a destination. In this turbulent and digitally infused environment, the customer has returned into focus for companies not just because he or she is the one paying for your product or service and is able to scream and moan online if you do something bad in their eyes. Customer-centricity is important because it's the most effective way to break down an enterprise's antiquated silo structure. That's why more and more companies are articulating their transformation around the customer. Yet, as we established in the last chapter, the route to a great customer experience happens through the employee. If you really want to create (or optimize) the best experience, you will need to have an organized, synchronized and motivated team.

As leaders today, part of our challenge is to figure out which path to take, given the innumerable choices and ever-limited resources. Furthermore, the context in which we're operating is more transparent, faster paced and with considerably more data sources and points of contact. Especially with the new technologies at our disposal, there's an inevitable pull to zero in on the consumer. Back in the noughties, when I started consulting with companies and proposed activities that put the customer at the heart of their strategy, executives would furrow their brow as if to say 'duh, of course'. In one instance, however, I can vividly recall when I asked the board of directors of a large bank to get into the shoes of the customer, the CEO himself asked out loud, 'But, how do I do that?' He came to the stark realization that it was foreign to him. It was this *a-ha* moment that made the entire day worthwhile. In reality, most companies have had their eyes knocked off the ball, besieged by the new environment and disoriented by the need for a new mindset. As the last decade progressed, executives started to understand that being customer-centric wasn't just about ensuring that the customer was satisfied. Being customer-centric is also fundamental to helping ignite and orient the required business transformation.

In fact, as we stand today, a majority of companies have pushed customer-centricity up as one of their strategic priorities, sometimes in the guise of improving the customer experience. This is supported around the world and in different industries. In the global survey by Adobe and Econsultancy of around 13,000 marketing, creative and technology professionals, published in 2018, they found that 45 per cent of respondents ranked customer experience and content management as one of the top three priorities.[1] In their 2019 version of the report, optimizing customer experience ranked second in terms of strategic objectives.[2] And if there's one obvious conclusion about the digital transformation process, it is that transformation mandates a return to the focus on the customer. Moreover, a survey by Econsultancy established that for 58 per cent of respondents, being customer-centric was the most important trait for establishing a truly 'digital native' culture.[3] If your company isn't genuinely organizing itself around the customer, there's a major chance that it will become yet another casualty of the new digital era. As a stark warning, the stakes have risen because now most companies are *saying* they are customer-centric. But who's doing it best? The question is: How and where will the rubber hit the road?

It seems that every other company or store front I turn to has some kind of communication implying that I, a potential customer, am the most important stakeholder. At the head of all companies today, under the ever-obsessive Jeff Bezos, Amazon has made its main mission and mantra 'To be the most customer-centric company on Earth'. In the travel sector, the British-based TUI uses the slogan 'We cross the "T"s, dot the "I"s, and put "U" in the middle'. Again in the travel space, Monarch Airlines used the slogan 'Fly *your* way every day'. Many banks, in the face of a generalized public mistrust, trot out that they believe they exist to make the customer satisfied. For example, Wells Fargo writes on its website, 'Our enduring vision is to help our customers succeed financially'.[4] I don't know about you, but I feel that the vast majority of the traditional banks have fallen well short of the mark.

In the beauty world, L'Oréal's famous slogan for the past near half-century has been, with a few tweaks, 'Because I'm [now *you're*] worth it'.[5] Canon's slogan (only in Asia) is 'Delighting *you* always'. Samsung has used the 'Digitally Yours' signature. The defunct Kodak used 'You press the button, we do the rest'. Burger King, which changed its slogan in 2014 from 'Have it your way' to 'Be your way', has embraced the movement to lifestyle. Compaq asked, 'Has it changed your life yet?' Yahoo! used 'Do you Yahoo?' Not only are many companies now brandishing that the customer is important, it's hardly a new concept. Marks & Spencer boldly launched a slogan in 1953, 'The customer is always and completely right!' However, as the fortunes of several of these companies mentioned above attest, just because you say it, doesn't mean you do it and certainly doesn't guarantee success. Moreover, many insiders and customers alike would agree that the customer experience doesn't live up to the promised billing. A 2014 report by the CMO Council in the United States said, 'Only 14 per cent of marketers say that customer-centricity is a hallmark of their companies, and only 11 per cent believe their customers would agree with that characterization.'[6] It's more than likely that the situation hasn't improved much since 2014 because the landscape and expectations keep on changing.

The customer-centric mindset

From a top-line level, a customer-centric organization is one that pursues actions that build trust with – and provide value to – the customer. As a leader, you will need to set the example of what customer-centricity looks like for your brand. For each industry and depending on the existing culture and history of your company, there will be no *best* practices to copy from. There will only be *better* practices, that's to say those activities, behaviours and attitudes that are better aligned to your situation and strategic intentions. That said, there are some important principles that underlie the way YOU LEAD an organization centred on the customer. The first is to establish, with honesty, just how focused on the customer you plan to be. Reality is that there is a scale and many variables and inputs will cause your form of centricity to differ. For example: To what extent are you prepared to sacrifice short-term gains for your customer's greater satisfaction? How will you arbitrate resources, where your own interests are appropriately managed in pursuit of customer delight? How will you disperse the authority throughout the organization to operate in a way that serves the customer's interest? As brave as the M&S mission might have been, I prescribe a more nuanced approach whereby you need to take stock of who you are as a brand as well as your principles of governance (as we explored in Chapter 2). If your reputation is to be more focused on your product or profits, it will take a greater effort to move the needle up the customer-centricity scale.

In Figure 6.2, on the left-hand side, I show the different orientations that encumber a corporation from becoming focused on the customer. Many companies are still taking their main decisions based on profitability. Sales-oriented companies will look to drive top-line revenues. Both of these can be characterized as shareholder-first orientations. There are those that are obsessed by the product, typically because of the hegemony of the 'rational' or engineering mindset. When too much weight is given to product by R&D, for example, this can cause interference with getting the right inputs, services and communications with the customer.

Some brands fall into the trap of using marketing trickery and over-promoting and/or discounting their product offer. As a consequence, money is being diverted from creating value and there's none left over to spend on doing right by the customer. Others, for example pure-player e-commerce companies – or those with enormous prior investments in tech systems – may drive their decisions based on the existing infrastructure. Yet other companies will focus on logistics or operational efficiencies. Another orientation that inevitably occurs in multinationals is the employee focus on internal careers. This is when

FIGURE 6.2   Orientations that encumber customer-centricity

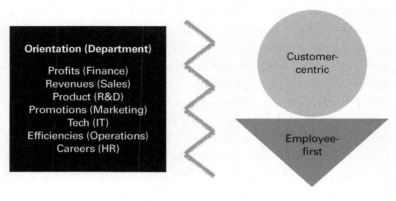

executives are keyed up on their next promotion. The culture encourages managing up and leaves room for infighting. For companies where the promotion 'calendar' means that executives move every three years, you're expected to make a splash within the first six months of arriving in order to confirm your new posting. In such situations, the executive can be more focused on undoing what his or her predecessor did or executing some bold decision with visible short-term benefits that could be at the expense, for example, of building a long-term relationship between the brand and clients. Parenthetically, such see-sawing can leave the remaining employees bewildered.

The column on the left in Figure 6.2 is not even a definitive list, as one can also find other constraints such as legal elements, not to forget the biggest hindrance of all: ego. While any company naturally needs to work on the items on the left, it's about magnitude and priorities. When the priorities aren't straight, the consequence is that the eye is taken off the ball of the customer. On the right, you have a customer-centric company balanced on the foundation of an employee-first culture. If neither is entirely stable, it's because you can never sit on your laurels and you have to earn your stripes on an ongoing basis.

A customer-centric mindset essentially means aligning the business around the customer. This will include the way the company is organized, reporting structures, staff rewards and remuneration. A customer-centric business is based on an employee workforce that is motivated to row in the same boat in the right direction. More than anything, it will involve shifting the culture of the business, including how you build up a network of reliable external partners. Importantly, when YOU LEAD an employee-first customer-centric business, what goes for or is promised to the customer must be relevant for the employee. To wit, there was a 2016 employee engagement study carried out by the Temkin Group that showed that companies that led in delivering the customer experience had 1.5 times as many engaged employees as those companies that trailed in customer experience.[7] There's a level of fulfilment that comes from accomplishing great service and doing so with a team of equally committed individuals. Of course, there's a chicken and egg story here. Is that employee engagement the consequence of delivering a great customer experience or because of the original re-cruitment and culture of the organization?

When YOU LEAD an employee-first customer-centric business, what goes for or is promised to the customer must be relevant for the employee.

Example of a customer-forgetful organization

Among the myriad examples of how to be *customer-uncentric* was the one demonstrated by Eurostar in the renovation of its high-speed trains, circulating between England and mainland Europe. In late 2015, with much fanfare, Eurostar rolled out new e320 wagons, built by Siemens (Velaro) and designed by 'the world-famous Italian design house [Pininfarina] that creates

Ferrari's unique style'.[8] The marketing brochures trumpeted improvements such as new seats, lighting, electronic signage and onboard wifi. Clearly, there were other more prosaic and justifiable corporate objectives, such as increasing capacity and efficiency. Specifically, the new wagons had a higher train load of 894 passengers versus a capacity of 750 previously. I was particularly excited about finally having the wifi. However, to call the connectivity spotty during the journey would have been a compliment.

The topic of wifi on board trains (whether subway or high-speed) is now a serious requirement from the passengers' perspective. The issue today is less technological than it is a question of prioritization (notably of resources). Learning to take on board such a functionality requires forcefully understanding the customer need (and anticipating it in the design process). For example, to what extent does senior management travel in the train as if a customer? Whereas management may have international phone contracts, many passengers and tourists may legitimately need an internet connection without racking up roaming charges. The technology exists for effective wifi in high-speed trains. But, as with any arbitration, does management wish to deliver on the customer experience or on the short-term bottom line?

What Eurostar also managed to overlook in the new design was the experience for getting on board, where the new steps on the e320 were sizably smaller, making it less safe for able-bodied passengers carrying luggage, much less safe for those with disability. When designers and engineers are not obliged to understand the customer experience, you will end up with a faulty product. And if the senior managers don't have empathy or walk in the passengers' shoes, you get decisions that are far from centred on the customer. In the case of Eurostar, the simple fix would have been to include staff and passengers in their design process.

Measuring customer-centricity

There's an adage that says: 'You can't manage what you don't measure.' But there's no easy answer to measuring customer-centricity. Would that there were some magical number that you could aim for in developing a more customer-centric organization! The first and most important task is to be able to describe the customer experience you wish to deliver and to derive meaningful insights from and about that experience. For example: Where and why are the magic moments? Where are the pain points? How are the pain points different for different types of people? Which customer journey has the highest conversion? Why is that the case? When and why do customers speak about their experience?

That said, businesses still need to find a way to measure their customer-centricity. There are those who would hang their hat on the Net Promoter Score (NPS), but as Adrian Swinscoe, an expert in customer experience, says, NPS is a measure, not a target. The reality of establishing an appropriate target must be related to your specific context and strategic imperatives. The dashboard that you use is entirely revelatory of your business's orientation. What numbers do you follow on top? What are the highlighted elements? How simple is your dashboard? How often and to whom is it circulated? Which customers do you follow? And, importantly, how are the key numbers tied into the rewards and recognition mechanisms of your company? I would go so far as to say that your dashboard reveals who you really are as an organization. If the customer isn't front and centre on top of your dashboard, chances are that you are far from being customer-centric. Meanwhile, a 2016 Forrester report on customer experience showed that brands that deliver a superior customer experience drive nearly six times more revenue than their competitors.[9] And according to Deloitte Research from the same year, companies that are customer-centric will drive 60 per cent higher profits than those that aren't concentrated on the customer.[10] In sum, being customer-centric is good for the top *and* bottom line.

The important thing is to make sure that the voice of the customer is being heard upfront and is integrated into the company's key performance indicators. At its heart, there needs to be a fundamental belief that customer success is tied to your own success. But part of the challenge of measuring the customer experience is that one must match up online data with offline information that will be in an analogue format, often reliant on manual inputs. Secondly, the information is inevitably spread throughout the organization with different stakeholders (eg third-party wholesalers) or in different departments (eg social media, customer service, sales, retail). For international companies with global customers, the challenge is to enable or enforce that business units share their customer data with one another. A fourth challenge lies around how the various moving parts of the company coordinate in the interactions with the customer along the various touchpoints. This requires skills, knowledge and attitude articulated around a shared strategy. It also requires a degree of flexibility and agency for the employees so as not to be over-policed and bogged down by policies and small print. All of these issues, walls and capability gaps make getting a single view of your customer difficult, much less managing the asynchronous, multi-platform, off- and online communications.

If you are serious about customer service for your business and genuinely wish to have supremely happy customers, there are myriad types of money-ball numbers you could use. The condition for establishing that singular number is that it is intimately related to your strategy. It also has to be congruent with your culture. For example, imagine your company's slogan is 'Get Inspired'. You decide that you want to make that inspiration materialize for your customers. You decide to set up a Get Inspiration Channel (GIC), providing original, inspirational and valuable advice. No strings attached. No product placement or pitch. It's updated daily and made available to all your customers for free. At the end of each inspirational asset, the customer clicks a simple feedback form that establishes how inspired they feel and the desire to do something positive. The corporate dashboard features the GIC score. Internally, you reward the team creating the daily inspiration that garners the best ratings. Of course, the data team is also sifting through the correlations to gain other insights and to see how GIC may be improving customer satisfaction. The net result ought to be increased inspiration which, if the strategy is right, will lead to greater sales.

In another case, if customer delight were your objective, you might measure the number of times that certain customers write in unsolicited compliments. You could also aim for zero calls coming into your customer care centre from a strategic segment of customers whose lifetime value is known and understood throughout the organization. But unlike companies whose objectives are confused and mixed in with conflicting financial targets, when YOU LEAD, you'll aim for such a target all the while, making your phone number blatantly obvious in all your communications and toll-free to call. Zappos is a brilliant example, providing exceptional customer service and implementing a customer-centric service. Moreover, to the credit of Amazon, which purchased Zappos in 2009, the company has been allowed the freedom to put this strategy in place with a specific organization and by enabling its employees. Zappos has a decidedly flat structure and the employees are given the flexibility to join the teams with which they feel an affinity. I am sure that such agency is vivifying.

Companies are clearly not being customer-centric when, for example, they:

- intentionally hide the customer service telephone number;
- put 'contact us' at the bottom of an endless scrolling web page;
- make customers connect through a form or channel that isn't the customer's preferred route;

- make it difficult to get through to a live customer service agent;
- reward customer service agents merely for the speed with which they handle enquiries.

Is your brand doing any of the above? When YOU LEAD a customer-centric organization, you start by walking in the customer's shoes. It's important that you lead by example. For instance, you call in from a number that won't be flagged as coming from a head office executive to live a customer's experience.

The role of data in the customer experience

If there's one thing that must be part of measuring your customer-centricity and the customer experience, it's data. Despite the publicity around big data, most companies are far from using their available data effectively. There are situations where companies have latched on to the data opportunity, but the challenge of developing and exploiting insights is encumbered by a culture that isn't focused on the customer. A customer-centric company knows that customer data and insights must be democratized, albeit in a safe and intelligent manner, across the organization. In the messiness of a multi-channel customer journey, one of the big challenges is assimilating analogue data along with the digital. This means, for instance, being able to collate employee feedback and customer feedback from the front line. Not only is including the voice of the employee likely to provide useful insights from the front line, employees are more than willing to participate, will enjoy being heard and will likely feel more motivated, especially if the company responds to and acts on their suggestions. The key attitude here is listening. But to

When YOU LEAD a customer-centric organization, you start by walking in the customer's shoes.

shift the culture requires a dogged determination and leadership by example.

With the intention to improve the customer experience and using a global and centralized perspective, McDonald's' former CEO Steve Easterbrook, before being caught up in a scandal and sacked in November 2019,[11] did some excellent work with his team in collating and assessing data, and bringing new technologies into its business. For example, using a global social media monitoring tool, they identified an opportunity to make changes in their menu, including making their breakfast available all day long and creating a healthier set of options. As one finds in all customer-centric activations, such efforts require a concerted and coordinated approach, involving in this case important changes to the supply chain, staff training and educating the customer, too.

Companies that are product-centric will pay an excessive amount of attention to their R&D and will tend to scoff at customer feedback as if they, the engineers or scientists with PhDs, always knew better. I recall how the R&D laboratories at L'Oréal used to resist our customer-based requests for hair styling products that made the hair purposefully dirty. Yet, it was an evident trend spearheaded by a competitor and the labs were too proud to ever admit that a competitive product was better or more innovative. Symptomatic of a product-centric mindset, the concept of dirty or undone hair was foreign to the way the L'Oréal scientists had been trained and it took an inordinate amount of time and effort to get them to finally come around.

The future of customer-centric data management

Personalization is a core concept for customer-centric marketing. But, as shown in the cycle in Figure 6.3, to get the personal data in order to provide relevant personalization requires permission. And deeper permission comes with building a corresponding trust. One of the core soft skills that can help you to garner

FIGURE 6.3   Virtuous or vicious cycle

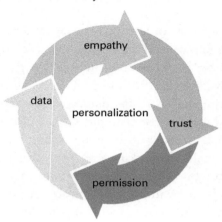

that trust is empathy. But, in a case of a virtuous or vicious cycle, to be good at empathy, especially at scale, requires an enormous volume of data. As I highlighted in my last book, *Heartificial Empathy*, data is the basic ingredient to help start to insert empathy into your customer interactions and artificial intelligence.

A new field of expertise in business: ontology

Looking forward to a more sophisticated management of data around the customer, where we've made progress in big data analytics and artificial intelligence, I can foresee some enlightened companies hiring a chief ontologist. According to Merriam-Webster, ontology is 'a branch of metaphysics concerned with the nature and relations of being'.[12] As such, it's about the essence of what exists, what is reality. Whereas much of our education is based on the study of knowledge (aka epistemology), ontology is more existential and philosophical. Yet, in the world of data management, it can have a decisive impact in helping to parse out data that is useful and making it relevant in the right context.

While ontology has generally been applied to the life sciences, in the context of business it has significance in helping to sort what is or isn't important. Academics such as the English mathematician and philosopher Alfred Whitehead and the Australian philosopher David Malet Armstrong held that the results of ontology could be evaluated only as a function of the overall system.[13] Meaningful data thus exists only in a context and a cultural system. The French consultant Alexandre Beaussier, with whom I've had the pleasure to work for over the last five years, describes the process as follows: 'Ontologies will make it possible to "connect" diverse and singular experiences together based on the concepts and ideas they have in common.'[14] Critical to this form of customer relationship management is understanding the human experience in his or her specific context. To be able to capture that context requires the building of confidence between the customer and the brand, but equally among the different stakeholders, such as the separate department heads, third-party suppliers and distributors. Beaussier continued that, in order to gain the most valuable insights, you'll want to 'use the data produced at each interaction in order to inform individuals and groups on the experience they are actually living and help them better navigate in the knowledge they developed through these experiences'. Inherent in this statement is the power of and need for ongoing learning.

The power of continuous learning

Leaders who want to create consistently superior customer experiences will need to evaluate and implement a new form of learning that includes the acceptance of mistakes. This doesn't just mean having an incessant curiosity. It means being prepared to dig into the messiness of the human context, including handling emotions, chemistry, errors and bugs. **When YOU**

LEAD, you will make clear the link between the strategic imperatives and the details and actions being executed on a daily basis. You'll be sharing the data and insights through the different strata of the company, and you'll need to be aware of the consequential changes in behaviours that such open access will require. For example, the teams will need to understand their responsibility in how they securely access and use the data. You'll also want to evaluate the capabilities and assess the ongoing training needs that not only 'teach' your team the right skills but motivate and spread the right attitude.

Putting the customer into service

In 2016, I wrote in a blog post that customer service was going to be the new marketing.[15] I believe this is even more true today. At some level, all of marketing must adopt a customer service mentality. Not only do marketers need to consider their work as being at the service of the customer, they must also want to work in unison with – sometimes at the service of – other parts of the organization. When I ran Redken Global, I used to talk about how the Redken subsidiaries were our customers. For some marketing-oriented companies where marketers tend to develop an oversized view of themselves, this can be a revolutionary point of view. The role and scope of customer service have been undergoing a seismic change. The channels have multiplied and transparency (eg through transcripts and recordings of the customer service interactions) has become an expectation. Worse, the customer – some more powerful than others – has firing power and an ability to call out bad service. Customer service has become absolutely strategic. And **if you want to be customer-centric, the customer service department is a great**

Customer service has become absolutely strategic.

place with which to start because it's systematically the only entity that actually has the word *customer* in its title. It's also a fount of information, with direct and free feedback from the front line.

Who owns customer service?

Insofar as customer service should, at the very least, be bonded with marketing, it can make sense to have customer service report into marketing, providing the governance is appropriate and the marketers doesn't try to use it as another marketing channel. At Glossier, the disruptive beauty brand that has made being close to the consumer a de facto mantra, the customer service agents are part of the operational marketing team and make the customer experience feel real by sharing personal stories with the customers. In another remarkable case, when Kevin Ryan was CEO of the luxury flash sale e-commerce site Gilt, he had every one of the 800 employees of the company go through two days of customer support training and spend time on the phones with customers.[16] This included his executive committee through to engineers and data scientists. In so doing, Ryan helped make his entire organization sensitized to the voice of the customer.

What does real customer-centricity look like?

When one says that beauty is in the eye of the beholder, one might also say that customer-centricity is in the eye of the customer. And it's a fickle and difficult challenge for any business, especially for legacy companies that have strayed from the customer. I would recommend you establish a list of companies whose customer service impresses you, no matter the industry. For example, were I to be managing a luxury brand today, I would certainly want to benchmark against Amazon. In order for you to appreciate to what extent you are part of a customer-centric organization, I have collected a number of observable behaviours, attitudes and activities that describe what customer-centricity does and doesn't look like.

Some examples of what customer-centricity doesn't look like

GOVERNANCE/ORGANIZATION

- Your board of governors has no one who represents the customer.
- Your organization is hierarchical, and you prefer a centralized approach.
- Your organization is structured around your product offer or distribution channels as opposed to customer type or journey.
- The P&L hasn't been adapted to reflect your customer-centric strategy.
- You defer only to the law to consider your ethical boundaries.

MANAGEMENT

- You have adopted the gimmick of the empty chair to represent the customer (first invented by Jeff Bezos), but it's often loaded with overcoats or only ever mentioned at the beginning of meetings.
- Top management rarely if ever eats with the rest of the employees.
- The executive team includes several people who have low digital IQs.
- On principle, the senior team doesn't use social media.
- The HIPPO principle, where the opinion of the highest paid person in the room holds most sway, exists.
- Vanity metrics – such as number of visitors, fans and likes – are still a topic of discussion.

- None of your top three performance indicators includes the customer.

HUMAN RESOURCES

- You've never discussed empathy as a strategic soft skill.
- Your Learning for Development department offers an annual curriculum that comes out in a printed format.
- You've not got customer-centric measurement criteria as part of the employee evaluation.

MARKETING

- You send out marketing messages that are not fully and appropriately personalized.
- You struggle to have an open rate of your CRM emails above 30 per cent.
- You don't revalidate the value of your communications with your customers, including a one-step top-of-page way to unsubscribe. Worse, you prefer to ask customers to opt *out* rather than opt in.
- Your FAQs are not customers' most frequently asked questions.

TECHNOLOGY

- Your IT infrastructure is too clumsy and slow to change in favour of an improved customer experience.
- You think of artificial intelligence as a way to cut costs or automate customer interactions.
- You operate with long-winded policies, too much small print and/or bureaucracy.

And here's what customer-centricity does *look like*

GOVERNANCE/ORGANIZATION

- Your company has a de facto purpose that goes beyond just serving your stakeholders. Your mission means providing a positive impact on the larger community.
- Your board of governors has a broad mixture of diverse perspectives, where everyone is equipped and encouraged to speak up and many of whom are in regular contact with customers. Even the governors think and feel in the shoes of clients.
- The customer-friendly CEO incarnates the brand, is the company's number one fan.
- The CEO's strongest asset is the ability to listen.
- Your board of directors embraces transparency.
- Your capabilities include talented customer experience analysts, data scientists and technologists with empathy.
- You've worked on an ethical framework with a diverse group of inputs that has a strong empathic fibre. It's broken down for all types of interactions, inside and outside the company.

MANAGEMENT

- The voice of the customer is present at every major decision.
- All your senior executives spend time listening to and engaging with customers on a weekly basis.
- Customer metrics include emotions and behaviours that are sourced across the largest possible array of inputs.
- Employees are recognized and rewarded for developing and delivering on deep customer insights.
- Empathy is a strong attribute among all senior managers.
- Curiosity and continuous learning are innate throughout the organization, starting at the top.
- Customer data is secure, yet democratically available, for all relevant staff to mine.

- You use artificial intelligence to augment human performance and increase employee fulfilment and engagement around the customer.

HUMAN RESOURCES

- Your employees are your company's top fans.
- Your employees gain personal fulfilment in a consistent manner aligned with the company's mission for customers.
- Employee targets and rewards are based on relevant strategic measurements tied to the customer, for example their lifetime value.
- The employee experience is measured as a key performance indicator (KPI) and is an important hook for recruiting new talent.
- Your employees have the training, agency and resources to deliver customer delight.

MARKETING

- Marketing works tightly with customer service.
- Every possible message to the customer is hyper-personalized and relevant.
- Messages to customers have headlines that are revisited dozens of time, each time, before being sent out.
- Open rates generally exceed 50 per cent and customers eagerly await the next message you will send them.
- Customers feel that the company has always got their back. For example, if the deal the customer bought isn't the best on offer, the company proactively provides the customer the more attractive option.

TECHNOLOGY

- The technology helps provide the best user experience.
- Sensitive customer data is protected.

- Following the Estonian model, the technology never asks twice for the same information.

BOTTOM LINE

- Customer lifetime value is common currency.
- Profitability is not a dirty word.

Recap of key messages and actionable points

- The very act of focusing on the customer is the most effective way to bring about transformation in your organization.
- The challenge of being customer-centric is that it is not an objective but a mindset. Considering the human involvement throughout a mixture of off- and online channels all along the customer journey, when YOU LEAD you will want to embrace, enhance and elevate the employee experience at each stage.
- When YOU LEAD an employee-first customer-centric business, what goes for or is promised to the customer, must be relevant to the core for the employee.
- The important thing is to make sure that the voice of the customer is being heard upfront and is integrated into the company's key performance indicators.
- When YOU LEAD a customer-centric organization, you start by walking in the customer's shoes.
- When YOU LEAD, you will make clear the link between the strategic imperatives and the details and actions being executed on a daily basis.
- Customer service has become absolutely strategic. And if you want to be customer-centric, it's a great place with which to start because it's systematically the only department that actually has the word *customer* in its title.

Endnotes

1. https://wwwimages2.adobe.com/content/dam/acom/au/landing/DT18/ Econsultancy-2018-Digital-Trends.pdf (archived at https://perma.cc/7CCZ-DLDM)

2. www.adobe.com/uk/modal-offers/article-digital-trends-2019.html (archived at https://perma.cc/TJZ8-ZSME)

3. econsultancy.com/what-are-the-key-digital-strategies-for-2016-stats/ (archived at https://perma.cc/UL9G-KL32)

4. www.wellsfargo.com/about/ (archived at https://perma.cc/EB4B-X68A)

5. www.lorealparisusa.com/about-loreal-paris/because-youre-worth-it.aspx (archived at https://perma.cc/3XAJ-LZ9J)

6. cmocouncil.org/thought-leadership/reports/mastering-adaptive-customer-engagements (archived at https://perma.cc/J3H5-LKQQ)

7. https://web.archive.org/web/20200526045551/https://experiencematters. blog/2016/02/16/report-employee-engagement-benchmark-study-2016/ (archived at https://perma.cc/48WK-NBQM)

8. www.eurostar.com/uk-en/about-eurostar/our-company/our-new-trains (archived at https://perma.cc/TCP4-RZGZ)

9. go.forrester.com/blogs/16-06-21-customer_experience_drives_revenue_ growth_2016/ (archived at https://perma.cc/L253-ACF7)

10. www2.deloitte.com/content/dam/Deloitte/de/Documents/WM%20 Digitalisierung.pdf (archived at https://perma.cc/8UJV-YCPF)

11. www.bbc.co.uk/news/business-50283720 (archived at https://perma.cc/ E6H2-TEGP)

12. www.merriam-webster.com/dictionary/ontology (archived at https://perma.cc/ JN5F-RKTS)

13. www.britannica.com/topic/ontology-metaphysics (archived at https://perma.cc/ 7Z4B-UYAQ)

14. Email exchange with Alex Beaussier, partner and head of innovation at SBT Human(s) Matter, a global cognitive design company

15. www.minterdial.com/2016/01/customer-service-is-the-new-marketing/ (archived at https://perma.cc/643V-F95E)

16. www.leadersmag.com/issues/2012.1_Jan/ROB/LEADERS-Kevin-Ryan-Gilt-Groupe.html (archived at https://perma.cc/G7FG-P6KT)

PART THREE

The challenges and realities of implementation

The personal journey

I write from personal experience. It was not a straight line to get here and I certainly erred and made many mistakes along the way. I, too, got buffeted and harried by time and my emotions. I carried masks, got some ideas wrong, made some comments to members of my team I shouldn't have. I even had terrible screwups. I remember one dreadful experience near the beginning of my time at L'Oréal. I was standing in the middle of the 'Salle de Confrontation', a conference room set up like a gladiatorial war room in Clichy, and I addressing the CEO and a coterie of L'Oréal's senior executives seated around me, a step up in a 360-degree circle. Very soon after having got the first few memorized lines out of my mouth, I completely froze and forgot what I was saying. It was an out-of-body experience. I was overcome with a horrendous feeling of humiliation and failure. In the pinnacle moment, in front of all the top brass, my boss and many teammates, I crashed. It was a lonely moment. This episode has never been lost on me now that I'm a professional speaker.

We all have to go through our own upsets and crises, just like any kid learning the power of fire. I'll also never forget the kind words of one executive who came up to me and compassionately said that I'd get over it. It's events like these that help build one's resilience. Aside from anything else, I learned how to prepare myself better for the L'Oréal style of slick speeches that were expected of the 'high potentials'. Three years later, on September 11, as I stood transfixed by what was going on outside my office window in Manhattan, another resolve kicked in. My resilience was far greater because I felt that, running Redken and living with my family in the heart of New York, I was in harmony with myself. It may have been turbulent, but I was doing and living something that mattered to me. It was a transformational moment. It gave me the fortitude to battle on.

Standing on stage in Paris, a week later, on the morning of 18 September 2001, I delivered a two-hour speech about the future of Redken, Fifth Avenue NYC, to a room packed with around 500 of L'Oréal's top executives, including the CEO. I gave what I feel was perhaps my finest performance, even though it was messy. Or perhaps because it was messy. Normally, this was a speech delivered by 12 members of my team in a highly choreographed manner. For this presentation, my team supplied me with all the information and slides I needed. On the lonely flight over in a private jet hired especially for this occasion, flying out of Islip airport on the morning of Saturday 15 September on what was purportedly the first non-military plane to fly in New York's airspace since 9/11, I had to learn the text by heart. This speech was to provide all the top L'Oréal brass around the world the confidence to invest in Redken in their country for the coming years. For me, meanwhile, at a meta level, it was about demonstrating the New York spirit. I felt the need to give a speech that was genuine and forceful. Back in Manhattan, I still had four friends missing. I had had to ask our graphic designer to retouch two of our 2002 advertising images to render the iconic twin towers less recognizable in the background. The first five minutes of the speech I completely ad-libbed. I knew my stuff. I had a great deal more confidence in myself and dominated my content. The rest was a show. I may have had a few wobbles, but instead of getting worried, I took them in my stride. It was a moment that I shall not forget, ever.

One of the core tenets of this book is that great leadership is a personal endeavour. That is to say that it is personal and professional. As a great friend of mine reminded me, if you don't think it's personal, check out the number of retired executives who feel lost without their job.

Considering the number of hours one spends at work, you ought to want to make it personal, otherwise, life might just pass you by. But, let me be perfectly clear: I don't subscribe to making work everything. This becomes all the more absurdly apparent when you retire: who are you, and what are you going to do with your time, if you don't have work? Some will just continue to 'do' stuff because the void is too big outside work. It's absolutely essential to cultivate your hobbies, spend quality time with yourself and those close to you, unfettered by work concerns. In these non-professional moments, the brain is still ticking over. Experiences, serendipitous encounters and quiet moments will surreptitiously nourish your work. The cult of overwork, not to mention the pressures of office facetime, are neither desirable nor sustainable. Where work becomes more energizing is when you feel the overlap between your personal and professional essence, aligned with your North Star setting. It's in this context that I pitch the notion of taking your work personally. If work can be fulfilling at a deeper level than just the title and pay cheque, then work starts to give energy back to you. Today, however, there are still plenty of executives who think that they can repress the personal side and focus only on the rational, unemotional side of work and performance.

I recall an instance in my career when a boss told me not to take his harsh criticism personally about a strategic note that I had written over the weekend and submitted to him for his approval on the Monday morning. I was floored. First, I reeled from the intentionally severe language. His language included terms like 'That was really stupid' and 'You have to be naïve'. Behind the words was a condescending and imperious tone. He told me again at the end, 'Of course, don't take this personally', as if everything were justified in a professional setting. What confused me entirely was not so much the underlying criticism (although it was hard to focus on the substance considering the style), it was that I thought that he'd want me to take my work seriously and personally. It's not an attitude you turn off and on. It's about being YOU. I can appreciate that he thought he was sharpening up my resilience, but in one's exuberance to impress and impose, you can also squeeze out any sense of belonging or positive respect.

In another instance, I remember how a boss humiliated one of my direct reports to such a degree that he made the 30-year-old man cry. After the dressing down, when the direct report had left the office, my boss defiantly indicated how part of his 'performance' had been for my own good. As in: he wanted to show me how I should manage people. I'm in favour of tough love, but there first has to be the love to allow for toughness. A third manager once advised me that I didn't hammer the table enough with my fist to affirm my authority. He literally pounded the table as he told me. The notion of having to be hard-nosed and authoritarian is not only passé, it's a sure-fire indicator of something wrong with the boss.

It was these very same individuals who were exhorting us to put in more effort, to perform, to be more creative, to be more entrepreneurial and to treat our budgets as if they were our own. I believe you should want your team to take it personally. This doesn't mean bringing all your personal issues to work or crying at every misstep. I'm not advocating for everything being ONLY personal. But it does mean taking into consideration each of your strengths and weaknesses, understanding the context of each person with whom you're dealing and, when needed, flexing your empathic muscle. When you are engaged in a long-term relationship, such as working with teammates at your company, you need to focus on the *how* as much if not more than on the *what* you are communicating. It sounds obvious, but many 'old school' executives were brought up believing in the combative interview to see how candidates would stand up under pressure. Their internal narrative was: that's how I was treated, so I don't see why I shouldn't do the same to the newbies... However, the leader of tomorrow is someone who doesn't feel the need to reproduce the old model.

In fact, the new leader is able to bring a whole unique form of leadership because it is sculpted around yourself. You need to be the best version of you. There is no one who can be you better. There are many imposters and inauthentic impersonators of leaders. The best leaders, those who are going to bring out the best in themselves and the teams around them, are those who are self-aware, understand their strengths and weaknesses and are prepared to be a truer version of the self. No one gets it right all the time, and it's not desirable or realistic to seek a perfect truth. When you accept your own failings, you'll be better able to live with the messiness and imponderables of life. You'll know that mistakes and failure are a part of learning and growing, and that a slightly imperfect product delivered on time is better than a concept stuck in the mind trying to be perfect.

The leader of tomorrow is someone who doesn't feel the need to reproduce the old model.

The leader who is able to embrace his or her imperfections is the one who will most likely inspire sustainable and healthy success.

To this point in the book, we have looked at the context in which leaders must operate and the principles of being a great leader. We've checked out the role of governance and how it can condition or limit your freedom to lead as you wish. We've established the strategic priority to create employee-first customer-centricity, discussed the required mindset, addressed the five key qualities (CHECK) and explored the nuances of leading an employee-first customer-centric organization.

In this third and final section, we are going to look at the specific leadership skills and practices, starting with the art of *being* a leader, no matter the size of the company or the industry. I'll finish with a set of practical ideas that can help you reconfigure your way of working, to adjust to the needs of today's seemingly manic existence.

The following two chapters (Chapters 7 and 8) are focused on the practical realities of a 24-hour day and establishing some behaviours that can help bring these principles to life, all the while making sure to stay true to yourself. The chapters deal with the most important resources you have at your disposal: yourself, your time and your people. With these resources, it's about optimizing your communications and how you will keep growing. One thing that tends to be a feature in each resource is the presence and role of digital. The tools we have at our disposal are vast and fabulous… for the most part. They can also be at times invasive and corrosive. It depends how you use them, of course. But we need to be highly self-aware to notice how our behaviours, moods and relations are being impacted by these digital tools, devices and platforms.

For each of these categories, I'm sharing the best tips and tricks – analogue and digital – that have worked for me. You are free to pick and choose whichever you like. I don't intend to be totally prescriptive because it will depend where you sit in your personal journey. Each of us has different prerogatives and styles.

CHAPTER SEVEN

The art of being a leader

CHAPTER OVERVIEW

We're all competent at creating lists of things to do, filled with timelines and priorities, and we all relish crossing off completed tasks. However, we're less good at filling in who we want to be. It's like the difference between achieving success and creating significance. When you create a fulsome North Star, you'll be better equipped to manage your time, accept the need to put your ego aside and lead from within.

Being: the power of being versus doing

Kick off with mindfulness

As much as it may seem counterintuitive, in order to adapt to the velocity and volume of change, I set down some routines at the beginning and end of the day. I think of it as a way to set a solid platform for my day. Every morning, I start my day by doing a guided meditation. My preferred service is The 10 Minute Mind by Monique Rhodes.[1] Monique is a special person. Originally from New Zealand, Monique has two platinum-selling charity albums to her credit, toured with Chuck Berry and worked on a music project with the Dalai Lama. When I listen to Monique's voice and music, I feel like I'm listening to the Himalayas. With this practice, I've found it easier to find calmness when thrown into a tempest. As hiccoughs are bound to happen, in life as in business, being able to find an inner peace has helped me to weather the web of wicked curveballs. Being present with myself has been good for my spirit and it's been especially important when it comes to active listening.

There are plenty of other guided meditation services such as Headspace[2] (with Andy Puddicombe) or Petit BamBou (which is also available in French with musician and friend, Ludovic Dujardin).[3] The second thing I like to do upon rising, inspired by US Navy Admiral McRaven's commencement speech in 2014, is make my bed. I do this even when on the road, staying at a hotel.[4]

Check in with your North Star setting

As I come out of my morning meditation, I consider my day and how I'm going to be in line with my North Star setting. Of course, I'm going to think of what I'm *doing*, but I want it to be intentional and related to my *raison d'être*. I've been doing this for over 10 years, so it's now become an ingrained habit. If you're keen to follow suit, I suggest you start by printing out your North Star setting and fixing it in a prominent place so it will remind you to do the same. For me, the biggest piece of the puzzle has been how to work on my self-awareness and where I have stumbled. We (and I can say 'I') have a habit of always considering ourselves above average, on everything. It's how high-potential individuals tend to be identified and groomed. Yet the law of averages would suggest that we can't all be above average.

A healthy mind in a healthy body

Would that we could all have healthy bodies until our last breath. Alas, that's not my case, nor is it for most of us as we age. Nonetheless, I've long maintained a practice of working out three to four times a week. Here's my routine: get my cardio up over 150 beats per minute three times during at least 30 minutes of hard pedalling on a stationary bicycle. I also tune my upper body and stomach area. As a complement to these workouts, I walk up to one-and-a-half hours every day.

Being fit is a commendable virtue as a leader.

My trick is to schedule in a walk between meetings rather than take public transportation (I don't own a car) whenever possible. I use the time to consume podcasts, all the while observing the cityscape and what's happening in the streets. It'll take a little longer, but it's a refreshing experience that feeds my soul.

Last, but not least, you have to eat well. As the politician Jean Anthelme Brillat-Savarin (of course, he'd be from France) wrote in his book, *The Physiology of Taste*, 'You are what you eat.'[5] While charcuterie and red wine don't sound healthy, there's plenty of research to show how the traditional French diet is not only tasty but good for us. The key is moderation. As leaders, we need to be holistic in our approach. If there's one personal thing that was always brought into the workplace during my time at L'Oréal, it was the pleasure of eating fine food. The importance of getting your energy right to equip yourself for the daily challenge cannot be understated. Notwithstanding the impact on your own longevity and the worrying issues of an overburdened healthcare system, it's literally daily fuel for your day. When YOU LEAD, you lead by example. Being fit is a commendable virtue as a leader.

Sleep

Along with the food (and drink) you intake, there's sleep. As I have written about in the past, sleep is one of the three most untapped levers of productivity at work (along with empathy and purpose). It's absolutely astonishing how, starting at school, we don't educate ourselves on sleep. When we sleep poorly, the impact is evident. We all inherently know that it will hurt our productivity, attentiveness, patience and sense of humour. But we continue to live in the proverbial dark, perpetuating myths and misunderstandings.

When I was at university, scouring for the selection of courses for the next semester, I fell upon a class in the brochure that was brand new. It was An Introduction to Sleep, taught by Professor Mark Rosekind, a young PhD student at the time who had to teach one class as part of his grant. It was, literally, an eye-opener. Aside from being a brilliant teacher, Rosekind raised our consciousness about the importance of sleep and corrected our misconceptions. Once I cottoned on to the relevance of the topic, I ended up taking all four available courses that dealt with sleep. In the 1980s, sleep as an academic topic was even more esoteric than my minor in Women's Studies. Today, there's no excuse not to devour any number of accessible resources to learn more about how you can sleep better. I believe that the Learning for Development centre in every company should include courses on sleep (alongside offering a comfortable place for naps on site). Aside from the practical matter of having people at work feeling more productive, it will materially help everyone's sense of self and health.

The art of conversation

Given our stressed, time-constrained lives, I see too many people who've lost the skill, much less the patience, for having a good, deep conversation. The sharp-toothed pragmatism of some bosses who feel it is their need to always be efficient, on message, singularly focused on productivity and performance is not only doing damage to themselves, it's going to hurt the long-term results of the company. A good conversation, that taps into important subjects, will not bear as much fruit as if it is entered into with openness of mind and empathy. Engaging in a good conversation is energizing for both parties. If you are entirely present during the conversation, listening intently and focused on expressions, emotions and non-verbal cues, you'll pick up so much more. Full-ranging conversations as I like to call them will bring up unanticipated thoughts and spur connections in the brain that we can't fabricate when left to our own devices. Furthermore, when you enter into such conversations, depending on your willingness to open up, you'll be learning about each other, giving yourself a chance to create a stronger bond and increase that most hallowed of leadership qualities: trustworthiness.

When you get confused...

Among my other daily habits, I make sure to include music every day. If I'm not singing a song and playing guitar, I make sure to listen to a half-hour of music daily while I work out, sit at my computer or during my walks. On special occasions, I will get to attend a live event – I've been to some 800 concerts in my life. Aside from the joy that music procures, it's a way for me to think differently. I think of it as an aeriation of the mind. Not that I can prove it, but I believe it contributes to a rewiring of my brain. And there's plenty of science that suggests that music works in and on many parts of the brain. Listening to or playing music is complex and requires many parts of the brain to work together to make sense of the sounds. If we want any chance to use a higher percentage of our brain, then we need to know how to access other regions of the brain and get those neurons fired up. When people talk about sex, drugs and rock'n'roll, it's far from a hapless coincidence. Music has its place alongside the other two because all three tend to activate multiple areas of the brain.[6] In a world of busy-ness, music is a welcome change of scene. How can you insert more music into your day?

Time: because it's your rarest resource

Many executives struggle with allocating their time. The evidence comes in many forms, including being frequently late to rendez-vous or meetings, regularly starting messages with the phrase 'Sorry for replying so late…', or feeling bad for encroaching on their personal time with the family and/or friends. Having to pardon yourself for not managing your time is a sure-fire indica-tor of difficulty in being strategic. **Either you are aware of what's important and therefore shouldn't be excusing yourself, or you're stuck trying to do too much because you've not made the tough decisions.** Some people might sheepishly raise a finger to say that when they excuse themselves, it's merely out of politeness. I call that out as being misguided and delusional. For starters, by arriving late, you are holding the others in less esteem. If it's just out of politeness, other people won't be duped. If you're always late, chances are that, over time, you'll attract people who tend also to be late. Bosses who imperiously say that it's OK for them to be the last one to arrive and expressly make all others wait at their expense are behaving in ways that suggest their staff are second-class people. For example, the excuse that the boss is working 'on more important things' suggests that the meeting in question isn't important enough. And, worse, such behaviour will ripple down and encourage others to operate in the same manner with their colleagues.

Since time is our rarest resource, it is incumbent on us as leaders to be rigorously strategic in how we manage it.

Gatherings: when you are face to face

As digital as life is and as convenient as it can be to digitalize things and communications, there's something entirely and inalterably human about meeting face to face. It's remarkable how many of the pure players are having to build out IRL components, whether it's Amazon setting up physical stores, Google creating outdoor advertising or Airbnb that actively encourages local meetups of its hosts. We can't rely only on digital connections and communications. The problem is that these IRL meetings will be more time-consuming. Moreover, they're generally messier and more unpredictable. Because that's the case, I believe it's important to set aside the time for connecting with people and allowing random conversations to flow.

Fifty per cent free

One of the most significant habits I developed as a senior executive was to block out half of my day and keep it free of appointments. It wasn't dogmatic, because we inevitably still have to cater to one or other boss's proclivities and demands. Yet I was adamant in protecting my time to avoid spending the day in back-to-back meetings. Aside from *meeting-itis*, where you end up holding meetings that come from legacy planning, you need to have enough free time to manage the unexpected events that reliably happen, to allow for strategic thinking and to meet your team members under different circumstances than merely in meetings. When you lead from the centre, you seek to meet up with people from all corners of your business, not just your direct reports. And you seek to do so in different settings. As a rule, I left my door open as much as possible during those 'unbooked' hours. But I would leave my door closed when I purposefully wanted privacy to work on a strategic note, for example. My wonderful assistant would guard my door preciously. If you want to be strategic in your work, you need to be intentional in the way you allocate time. It's no good saying that things overrun or are overwrought. They always do and always are. Unexpected events happen with such predictability, you need to anticipate them in your schedule.

Getting meetings right upfront

As for meetings, many businesses get this wrong. Some meetings serve a necessary purpose. But it's clear that many of them could be eliminated and the business wouldn't be the worse for wear. Meanwhile, for those that do have to happen, is the agenda clear and shared well in advance? Are the right people invited? Are they properly prepared? If these questions sound naïve, yet meeting-itis continues with abandon. The future of work calls for different measures and methods and, thanks to the new digital tools, we've got many new options available as well.

Unexpected events happen with such predictability, you need to anticipate them in your schedule.

When Bezos instituted the six-page memo system where the document is read out in silence by all participants at the start of every strategic meeting, the key notion that underpinned this method was preparation. In the same way that a slideshow presentation should serve as a support for illustrating a point, meetings need to serve a purpose. I think of how certain educational establishments have changed the way physical classes are run. Rather than go and listen to a professor give a lecture in a classroom, students are invited to do the reading and watch the lecture in advance. When they come to the classroom as a group, the purpose is to discuss together, a far more intuitively social exercise that will radically enhance the learning experience.

When YOU LEAD, you recognize that time is sacred. Make sure that the meetings you run or attend are strategic, that the purpose of the meeting is clear, the agenda is prepared in advance and the right people are invited and prepared.

Board of Governor principle

I learned this Board of Governor (BoG) principle of running meetings while at Redken. The idea is that, as in a boardroom constituted with engaged governors, everyone who is in the meeting is given equal weight. Everyone is allowed to comment on every subject, no matter their position or expertise. For example, if you've invited your financial director to the marketing meeting, they have the full authority to comment on each marketing campaign, not just in terms of the financial aspects of the initiative but on its marketing merits. If someone attends, they should have permission to participate in all topics, not just the one indicated for them. The idea is that everyone in the room should feel involved in each topic. Otherwise, you're wasting *their* time. Naturally, the idea isn't to speak for the sake of speaking out or trying to capture the boss' attention. Such interventions need to be cut in the bud. You must be a steward of your employees' time.

You must be a steward of your employees' time.

As for other principles that make sense as chairman of a meeting, I would highlight the ability to do four more things:

1 Make sure people are held responsible for their time – including yourself.
2 Bring all people in the room into the conversation as much as possible. Because of the nature of how people observe hierarchy, you need to make sure to listen openly and intensively. The optimal position is when you connect the dots, ideas and people.
3 Make sure that people are held accountable for their statements and promises, including attributing themselves roles and deadlines for each initiative or decision.
4 Be demanding about smartphone etiquette, starting with yourself. My rules are: No mobile phones on (or under) the table. All phones on silent. Only pre-identified calls are acceptable as interruptions.

I've seen many a manager frown or get irritated by co-workers sneakily reading their smartphones and then doing it themselves. It takes discipline, but a meeting in real life demands being present.

Colour-coding

With an electronic calendar, it's easy to attribute colours to different types of meetings, locations or activities. Colour-coding helps to visualize how strategic you are in your time management. Accordingly, I have specific colours for what's important to me. For example, I colour-code when I'm in Paris (yellow). I use orange for my international travel and brown for my podcast interviews. I have my activities and deadlines related to my publications in dark grey. And then I reserve green for the most important one as I'll elaborate below.

What are the important signals you can colour-code in your calendar?

People: leading from within

Lead with the why

As leaders, we are generally in a position of 'managing' people. When you're leading from within, from the centre, it doesn't mean you're discharged from responsibility. To the contrary, you're responsible all the time, in all interactions, off- and online. This underlies why you need to accept being yourself and presenting your personal side along with your professional one because you can't adopt an always-on professional demeanour that feels authentic for those by your side. In any event, a key responsibility of a leader is to help everyone in the team know why they are doing what they are doing. How is what they're doing – the project they're working on – linked to the company's strategy? How explicitly do they recognize the connection between their role and the company's mission? Sometimes you do need to give orders and take tough decisions, but you need to accompany those directives with an explanation of *why*. It will help craft greater meaningfulness and a sense of accomplishment when projects are finished, or goals are achieved. It bonds them to the organization and the company's purpose. Leaders do not survive alone. They know how to make a collective intelligence emerge. You need your team and they need to know it. That can take showing a degree of vulnerability. Yet when you ask for help or knowingly delegate authority, you are not relinquishing your responsibility. You need to take ownership and, if it errs, own up to your part of the fault.

Feedback

Effective and regular feedback is a necessary part of great leadership. In the previous chapter, I recounted a few ways how not to provide feedback. My first encouragement to you is to seek out feedback for yourself. If you show yourself open to receiving criticism, it will do two things: 1) you will get some insights and pointers that, as you see fit, can help you to improve; 2) it will sensitize your teammates to the difficulties of giving feedback and thus becomes a coaching opportunity in reverse. The key notion of feedback is to link the commentary to specific behaviours. If you can expose yourself to feedback from those around you, lean in when it comes to criticism that you don't like. Don't automatically defend yourself or dismiss it. As a way to materialize feedback, the key is to demonstrate you've taken on board the criticism through a change in behaviour. You may not have an immediate idea of how to manifest such a change but make it explicit to others once you have. As studies have shown, when you say something out loud, you tend to own it more. It emboldens your commitment.

If taking feedback can be difficult, giving it in a timely and empathic manner is a *sine qua non* function of great leadership. Naturally, you can't say one thing and do another. Whether it's in an informal or formal process, it behoves the leader to adapt one's style to the listener. I like to say that intelligence is about making sense. It's as important to make sense of what you hear and see as it is to communicate clearly in a way that the listener understands. It's necessarily a two-way street.

In all the years that I've been practising *giving* feedback I've learned five things:

1 It all begins upstream. If you've not provided clear, observable and mutually understood objectives upfront, you're likely to derail. When giving objectives, validate that your report comprehends in a frank conversation. Where are the measurable elements? What are the accompanying conditions for success? What happens if the goals aren't met?

2 When in doling out criticism to an individual you feel a little rush of emotion going on inside, it could be a good indicator of something else going on. There's a handy little reminder: when you point a finger at someone, there are three fingers tucked into your palm that are pointing back at you. Check to make sure that the criticism doesn't come from a bad place or conflict within yourself.

3 It's time to flex your empathic muscle. Especially when giving the feedback in a formal setting, in the quiet of your office, take the time to reflect on how the feedback will be received by the individual in question. Think through the context of the individual, what has been his or her journey for the year, and what are his or her expectations? What is their psychological profile? There are many interesting models, such as MBTI, DISC and Insights (my personal favourite), that can help to identify personality types. According to the system with which you're most familiar, it's a good way to consider how to deliver the feedback. For example, if they're

a dominant 'blue' (eg analytical, task-oriented) personality, it is important to be factual, precise and concise.

4 Particularly in formal evaluations, I prefer to have the individual speak first. Once they've had a chance to speak, not only have they perhaps cleared their chest, there's a chance they will be more present for what you have to say. The key here is to listen actively, with an open chest.

5 When it came to my turn, I formulate the positives first with points to encourage and upon which to expand. When it comes to discussing areas for improvement, it's always better to use specific and detailed examples to help illuminate your point. In conclusion, you might want to ask how they plan to change their behaviour in the future. As a method of encouraging the right mindset, a good question to ask of your teammate is how she or he might be able to expand her or his network in an effort to complement them, learn more and improve in the identified area.

A final word on feedback: never wait until a year-end interview to provide feedback. Organizations that focus on year-end interviews for their salary reviews need to adapt to make feedback an ongoing process, such that the year-end meeting is just a continuing conversation and affirmation without major surprises. I will never forget the instances when, waiting for my own review with the boss, I had absolutely no idea what he or she was going to say. Aside from being an indictment on unpredictable and unreadable executives, this is no way to construct a healthy dialogue. It's another unnecessary way of imposing authority and generating fear.

Reward, recognition and compensation

I constantly marvel at how people overlook the easiest of ways of motivating team members: to acknowledge them and say *thank you!* It happens so infrequently that you'd think it were a rare commodity, as if by saying it too often might possibly dilute its worth. Fear not. The only caution is not to thank someone if you don't mean it or the action done was not up to the expected standard. I'm certainly not one to give away awards to every kid that entered a competition. It takes away from the value of excellence, the one who performed and achieved to a higher level. Yet recognition and reward can also be widened to include other achievements. From the polite and considerate 'thank you' after someone does you a small favour to writing a thank-you note after a kind invitation, it's a healthy habit to inculcate from the start. Studies show that middle managers are better equipped with higher emotional intelligence than those at the top. As people rise up the hierarchy, they become empathically challenged and their emotional intelligence becomes swamped with over-rationalizations, pretension and a disposition that seems to prefer perfection over reality.

A sterling example I'd like to share comes from a CEO who would regularly invite to lunch an individual from any part of the organization – no matter the level – for having done something exceptional. Such rewards are priceless. Sure, there's a cost in terms of your time (and the bill for lunch). But the effect of such an action goes well beyond the recognition of an individual. If you want it to be truly effective, you might encourage others to recommend people to you so as not to fall prey to favouritism or misguided personal preferences. Another positive example I encountered was at a law firm in the West Country in the UK where the CEO got into the habit of writing personalized thank-you notes to his colleagues and employees. It was only when he started using cards with a bit more personality on the cover that the co-workers started pinning up their cards, to bear witness to their achievement. This behaviour – set by the top – was a concrete and visible demonstration of values that the law firm wished to live up to: friendly, honest and supportive. I'd point out that this law firm also developed a mission that went well beyond its bottom line: how to be proud of and develop the West Country counties where its employees live. Proof that any type of company can create a meaningful purpose.

Among the ways that kill initiative outright is when the wrong people take credit for work done. In a 2019 survey performed for the BBC in the UK on ethical behaviour, 12 per cent of employees said that they had taken credit for other people's work (15 per cent for men and 9 per cent for women).[7] Those figures are surely understated. The issue is typically at the top when a senior executive takes the kudos when all the real work was done down in the ranks. When YOU LEAD, you are the first to recognize and give value to others' good work, and you are prepared to call out others who take credit inappropriately.

The last point concerns remuneration. It's a complex issue, of course, and the cultural differences make this a subject worthy of a book by itself. But here are the conclusions I have made after my own experiences:

- Adopting a graceful posture, recognizing and thanking teams for their hard work, and providing meaningful rewards will develop far greater motivation than just higher pay.
- Don't skimp on the bottom ranks. If you want to have a motivated team and a satisfied client, you don't want to have the pay scale be a topic of discontent. The middle managers and people at the lower end of the organization are often those in contact and dealing with the customer. Further, if you believe that cutting back on employee salaries is a priority, then chances are you have other bigger issues to fix.
- If you have a meaningful purpose – one that truly goes beyond your company's immediate remit – the better the chances that you won't be forced to pay top dollar for the best talent. Working for a purpose is far more enlivening than a big pay cheque. Bear in mind that having a purpose is not an excuse for lower salaries, but when your stated *raison d'être* is a de facto reality, it can be a side benefit.

- When you consider incentives and bonuses, these are systematically going to be manipulated and gamed. That's the nature of them.

Conflict resolution

Managing friction, conflicts and differences of opinion is where the chaff is sorted from the wheat. As much as I have had a personal need to be liked (it's one of my weaknesses), I also appreciated people who spoke their mind and confronted my ideas. It's like receiving feedback you don't expect to hear. You need to be able to countenance differences of opinion. And conflict. While I may attribute many of the conflictual relationships I witnessed to miscommunication, over-sized egos and diverging objectives, the reality of limited resources and strategic management is that you need to embrace the tension that comes from having to reconcile conflicting opinions. I witnessed how conflicts tended to fester. When I was at Redken, we devised a specific roadmap to deal with conflict resolution. Here are the top-line principles:

- Whenever possible, focus on the shared strategic vision.
- Remove the ego.
- Always show respect. Listen intensely and don't cut the other person off.
- If a report comes to you about a conflict with someone else, the first port of call is to insist that they go back and iron it out between themselves.
- The 24-hour rule. When someone had an issue with someone else, we inscribed a 24-hour rule. This rule said that, as the 'offended' person, it was their responsibility to make the other person aware within 24 hours.

If it were in a meeting that the offence occurred, we encouraged the dispute to be aired in public, but if that didn't feel right or there wasn't time, the slighted individual had to flag it within a day. An email or text message was deemed an insufficient form of communication. A phone call or a face-to-face meeting was best. If not possible for acceptable logistical reasons, the two must agree to a mutually convenient time. If the affronted person didn't make the effort within 24 hours, he or she was bound to discard the issue. As a group, we then enforced that it could not be brought up again. This 24-hour rule was important because it also reflected the pace of business. This single rule encapsulated a key point: make sure your internal processes are aligned with your external business needs.

In essence, you develop a culture where people with a diversity of points of view are encouraged to disagree openly, even (especially) with you as the leader and/or chair of the meeting. This is a feature of the Board of Governors principle.

Open door/open chest

As top executives, our time is inevitably taxed. One of the diciest balances to hold is when and how to allow others to impose on your time. Your boss – especially if imperious – will put certain demands on your time. Meanwhile, as it pertains to allocating time to your co-workers, team members and partners, I like to encourage an open-door/open-chest approach. As I mentioned above, I would intentionally block out time in my agenda to account for unexpected events, for example when a report would come unannounced to my door. The more your door is closed, the more this interjection becomes hard for two reasons: a) the person coming in knows it is a disturbance, not to say a highly restricted privilege – this creates a build-up of stress that can be decidedly unhealthy for a decent exchange; b) you will need to switch on your empathic muscle with dexterity. Because you've created a closed-door habit, that means it can be difficult to master the mental gymnastics required to be open to the 'intruder'. Keeping an open door means that you are inviting interruptions. To the extent you set the tone and show that individuals must be respectful – in other words, they are knowingly responsible – you won't be invaded unnecessarily. Having an open chest and allowing for genuine emotions may be a messier process, but the alternative is a rational, inauthentic existence.

Recap of key messages and actionable points

- We need to be highly self-aware to notice how our behaviours, moods and relations are being impacted by these digital tools, devices and platforms.
- Being fit is a necessary virtue as a leader.
- Since time is our rarest resource, it is incumbent on us as leaders to be rigorously strategic in how we manage it.
- When YOU LEAD, you recognize that time is sacred. Make sure that the meetings you run or attend are strategic in nature, that the purpose of the meeting is clear, the agenda is prepared in advance and the right people are invited and prepared.
- If you find you're constantly apologizing for running late, either you are aware of what's important and therefore shouldn't be excusing yourself, or you're stuck trying to do too much because you've not made the tough decisions.
- You must be a steward of your employees' time.
- Unexpected things certainly happen with great predictability.

Endnotes

1. the10minutemind.com/ (archived at https://perma.cc/GQT3-HXLU)
2. www.headspace.com/ (archived at https://perma.cc/3NKZ-5UMQ)
3. www.petitbambou.com/en (archived at https://perma.cc/2SGB-J3MD)
4. www.youtube.com/watch?v=yaQZFhrW0fU (archived at https://perma.cc/Z3LM-3HFW)

5. Brillat-Savarin, J-A (1825) *The Physiology of Taste*, tr MFK Fisher,
www.penguinrandomhouse.com/books/18327/the-physiology-of-taste-by-jean-
anthelme-brillat-savarin-translated-by-mfk-fisher-introduction-by-bill-buford/
(archived at https://perma.cc/S7QK-EXGR)

6. For further reading, I'd encourage you to dive into Daniel Levitin's *This is Your
Brain on Music*, daniellevitin.com/publicpage/books/this-is-your-brain-on-
music/ (archived at https://perma.cc/E9BS-FU75)

7. www.bbc.co.uk/mediacentre/latestnews/2019/year-of-beliefs-morality-ethics-
survey-2019 (archived at https://perma.cc/N29B-D677)

CHAPTER EIGHT

Leadership in practice

CHAPTER OVERVIEW

Being a great leader means knowing how to communicate effectively, to wit the notion of being Chief Storyteller as the CEO. Communications are the lifeblood of an organization. However, the channels, platforms and codes of communications are constantly evolving. Moreover, speed and transparency are at a premium. Leaders need to move from being the know-it-all to a learn-it-all attitude as Microsoft CEO Satya Nadella says.[1]

Communicating: because communications are the lifeblood of the organization

During my time as a leader in L'Oréal, I was known to use email too much. As much as I tried to insist that I didn't always expect an immediate response, I still got criticized because others felt an unpronounced pressure to reply to the boss. I did believe that a response was due to my questions, but certainly not overnight. I learned to save and buffer my messages for work hours. I also strove to make my communications clear about my expectations. This might include adding a date or a confirmatory phrase such as: 'If I don't hear back from you, I'll take it that everything is clear.' However, inevitably, I wasn't always thoughtful enough and miscommunications and mishaps happened.

I felt that emails were exceptionally efficient as they provided an easy way to record and file exchanges. As opposed to an unannounced telephone call, you can choose when you reply to an email. Almost by definition, a phone call from the boss requires a more immediate response. For the majority of other calls, you can send through to voicemail, but that always felt like a clumsier approach. Today, I feel happier, if not vindicated, as people now call infrequently, even with other options such as FaceTime or WhatsApp. However, I've come to rethink the trade-off between efficiency and long-term effectiveness. Being a hound for efficiency means you may short-circuit some of the human wiring and connections.

If the variety of platforms has made messaging messier to handle, it's easy to set the notifications to your liking and it's easier to manage the communications in an asynchronous manner when you're ready. The big challenge is having the discipline and skills to do so. I have no bones with individuals who guard their private time at home or on holidays. In fact, all the more power to you, since it's not how I roll. I respect such a posture under two qualifications: a) When YOU LEAD, you've mutually agreed to clear time-delineated goals and objectives; and b) everyone knows to set up the appropriate out-of-office messages.

Communication is a fundamental skill to master. I will be forever indebted to the economist Lester Thurow whom I heard, during a speech while I was at university (*circa* 1985), say that he believed typing would become a vital executive skill.

Accordingly, with help from my dexterous mother, I learned to type at around 80 words per minute without error. If only I could learn to type as fast on the smartphone.

In a world where the number of communication platforms and devices has ballooned, the ability to stay on top of all that's being communicated has become virtually impossible. When you're looking to translate values into visible behaviours, there's a chance that it will involve, implicitly or explicitly, the way you communicate. You'll want to pay particular attention to promises made to serve your customer. For example, I've seen companies write on their social media page that they guarantee to reply within 24 hours. The challenge is making sure that the internal corporate culture is aligned to make that promise hold. If your company doesn't have a responsive culture within and among the staff, it'll be near impossible for the individuals manning the social media page to respond in a timely manner. I recall a situation where a social media manager (an intern) came to me frustrated that whenever she wrote a message to the communications manager in charge of the Labs, she'd never get a rapid response. When I quizzed the manager in question, she replied that she had better things to do than sit and watch her email inbox. Perhaps that was true, but her posture stood in contrast to the external promise. As a leader, you'll want to make sure that the internal communication patterns are aligned with the external promises and to model the necessary behaviour yourself.

Personal brand

Over the years, I have heard top executives vehemently defend both sides of the argument about having an active personal brand online. On balance, most CEOs today are only mildly or reluctantly present online. I believe this is an opportunity to be a standout leader. There are two main reasons for accepting not to promote your personal brand: a) you've got too many poor habits or things to hide; or b) you are chronically bad at following through and sticking with a programme. I believe it is now virtually a professional fault not to have some kind of presence online. I don't say that every leader needs to be active, but if you've got a good personality, you can do your company wonders by showing at least some of your personality online. The strict minimum is having an up-to-date LinkedIn profile. It's better than letting the web decide who you are on Wikipedia, for example. Secondly, by showing your personality, you are humanizing the brand. Moreover, by being present online as leader, you are implicitly giving permission and showing the way forward for your co-workers to do so as well.

As part of your personal brand online, I'm all in favour of letting your personality and your passions show through. I mentioned previously Verizon's Ronan Dunne who waves the Irish flag and openly supports the Irish rugby team. In one of the more unlikely examples of a senior executive creating a personal brand online, the burly 60-year-old CEO of a large mass retailer had a love of photography. When he dug in on the company's anaemic social media presence, he determined that he needed to set the example. With the help of his socially active daughter, he created an Instagram account where he exhibited his skill at taking aesthetic black and white photos with his Nikon camera. Quietly, his account started to gain traction and ended up with more followers than the company's account. The social media team was given the necessary impetus to create a more engaging and active presence online.

KEY INSIGHT

Whatever your passion, don't hesitate to let the cat out of the bag. People would rather do business over time with someone with passion rather than a soulless person. Express yourself!

It takes a while to find your voice and you do need to be judicious in the way you manage your online presence. But, for those of you who don't do it at all for fear of looking silly or doing something wrong, the bigger task is to look at yourself in the mirror and figure out how to move beyond those fears. Others will avoid being active online because they feel it's below their station or because they don't want to reveal any intellectual property. I am not promoting giving away the family secrets. But being active online and creating an authentic personal brand can also help reveal your company's culture and give an insight into the leadership philosophy. When done well, it's a way to express a domain expertise, even to be influential. If, for the rest of you, it's because you think you don't have time to do it, then I ask you: You don't have time to get in touch with or hear what your clients have to say? You'd rather other people (and media) manage your narrative and presence without your input? You don't mind if people searching for you fall on a homonym with an altogether poor image? And, finally, you don't have time to manage your long-term career, which could include working for another company in the future? Creating your personal brand online takes time. But it's a worthwhile long-term investment. You need to get ahead of the curve and put forward the best version of you, otherwise others will write their version of you for you.

Get ahead of the curve and put forward the best version of you, otherwise others will write their version of you for you.

As part of my own personal brand, ever since I left L'Oréal, I have implemented a self-imposed policy that involves making sure that I give away valuable content every day. This can be in the form of a blog post, publishing a podcast episode or writing an original tweet with an interesting link or inspirational quotation. Not only is this part of my personal brand, it's an integral part of my North Star setting.

> **KEY INSIGHT**
>
> When you do something that fits your North Star setting, you know why you are doing it, and this will give you back extra energy over and above the amount you expended doing it.

Storytelling

For those of you who came through marketing to your leadership position, you'll have no doubt about the power of stories. Storytelling is all the rage in marketing circles. However, it's somewhat of an arm's length activity when you are doing so for the brand. Between a lack of agency and laborious approval processes, corporate storytelling is often stiff and/or indistinct. It's a very different affair when you start telling *your* story. When I wrote *Futureproof* with my co-author, Caleb Storkey, we purposefully weaved personal stories into every chapter.[2] In *Heartificial Empathy*, I told the capital story of spending five full days with an empathic bot. In this book, I've interspersed personal stories to help bring some points to life. Storytelling can and should also be a part of our day-to-day activities. Yet it's not always obvious to bring storytelling into the workflow. Of course, I don't advocate constant storytelling. I do, however, suggest judiciously bringing personal storytelling into your narrative. Not only will it help you to be more convincing and memorable, it will inevitably provide a window into your personality.

> **KEY INSIGHT**
>
> When telling stories, make sure to add the personal touch, for example by expressing your genuine emotion or saying how the story personally impacted you.

Personal communications

A boss can no more delegate personal communications than their personal brand. Here are some tips and tricks to integrate into the way you communicate on a personal level via the different channels.

EMAIL IS A NECESSARY EVIL

Email is as yet a necessary evil, and it's cheap too. But for many people, it's all-consuming. For older members of the executive team, it's been a default tool for all their professional lives. An organization whose culture is predominantly on email is literally tunnelling itself into oblivion. We've now got a plethoric choice of new platforms and channels and, especially if you are working with freelancers, third-party suppliers, influencers or digitally savvy customers, you need to reconsider the way you manage your overall communications, including email. Your role as leader is to set the tone for how emails need to be managed. Be stingy in how many people you need to cc. Whenever you can, move people over to bcc, telling them that's what you're doing so they knowingly stop being part of the thread. And if email isn't where your customers hang out, you'll need to change channel quickly.

TEXT AND CHAT

Text messages and chats (eg Slack, SMS, WhatsApp) are by definition less formal and typically require more responsiveness. Depending on your digital hygiene, you'll want to indicate to others how you prefer to interact. For example, Sir Martin Sorrell (whose initials are SMS) was quick to say that he preferred text messages and, even during his reign as CEO at WPP, he was true to his word. He never failed to reply to my SMS. Especially if your workforce and customers slant younger, you'll want to be using chats and/or text messaging – including using whatever has come up latest. If you stop a channel, be sure to delete it so you don't end up with unanswered messages sitting idly there. Finally, although it's hardly strategic, I have come to learn to add emoticons, emojis and GIFs to introduce a little more playfulness. Let your hair down and give it a whirl.

SOCIAL MEDIA

Being highly active on social media is not a prerogative. But it's more than likely that you could be using social media to far better effect at a strategic level. Being totally off social media is only acceptable as a conscious choice. The key is to know which are the most relevant social media for your eco-system. You can ill afford to shun it if you wish to stay abreast of what's going on. I use LinkedIn and Twitter because I've learned to find tremendous value from them. I've curated my network and am disciplined in creating groups and streams to allow me to be effective and productive in a timely manner on the topics that matter. I encourage you to create groups and lists with specific people and targeted subjects to help make sure you can quickly read what is most important to you.

KEY INSIGHT

On social media, allow yourself to follow your personal passions alongside your professional needs.

NOTIFICATIONS

If time is important to you and you want to be good at communications, you will need to dominate your notifications – the alerts, banners and sounds you receive. It's stunning to see leaders whose mail or messages icons on their smartphone carry badges (the small red circle top right) with hundreds, even thousands of unread messages. I think of the enormous number of frustrated senders, whether they're clients, direct reports or simply friends and family. Some people may consider the high number of unread messages a badge of honour or will defend the situation with all manner of crafty post-rationalizations. However, I have yet to find someone with a visible badge problem who has a great mastery of his or her communications.

Having a serious approach to your communications means being up to date on a daily basis. Keeping those badges with unread messages is stunningly useless at best, and more likely pollutes your mind. If you like it that way, my recommendation would be to eliminate the badge notifications altogether. Second, in terms of allowing notifications to come through, you ought to parse carefully between messages you allow on your lock screen or in the notification centre versus those that appear as banner messages. When I come to the lock screen after a pause, I like to be able to scan the important messages I've missed. This means carefully vetting people from whom you receive notifications. Personally, for example, I allow the latest tweets from five very specific people I follow on Twitter. However, I am much more selective when it comes to the banner messages which appear at the top of my smartphone screen or on the top right of my desktop. For example, I don't accept WhatsApp messages to appear as banner messages, even temporarily, otherwise the top of my screen is worse than a rolling slot machine. Lastly, as a default, I categorically forbid anything to have a sound. First, it's yet another annoying way to get distracted. Second, more civically speaking, it's a distraction that impacts those around you, too. That's unacceptable behaviour.

Having a serious approach to your communications means being up to date on a daily basis.

ORAL COMMUNICATIONS

As a leader, you are always on display. Whether it's at the cafeteria, water cooler, smoking outside or just walking down the corridor, you are being inspected. Employees will look at you, even as you listen to and exchange with others. These micro-moments contribute to crafting the culture. You are setting an example that gets interpreted by them. You cannot control their thoughts or feelings. As long as you can acknowledge that you can't dictate the interpretation, your role is to impart an authentic and best version of yourself on an ongoing basis. I encourage you to bring your emotions, storytelling and personality to more interactions than you currently do.

Learning: because it's an ever-changing world

The last area of practical tips is on staying up to date. The issue is no longer about having the information. It's not even the knowledge. Both of these exist in abundance online. The real challenge, today, is how to parse through the noise, find the best sources for your needs and allocate the correct amount of time, such that you are effective and efficient in your work. Herewith are the tips and tricks that I have used to help me stay on top of the moving feast of technologies, skills, laws and practices.

Online learning

The amount of information available online is at once overwhelming and underwhelming. You can easily spend a crazy amount of time on YouTube and come away with nothing substantive. Online learning sites on specific topics, such as Coursera, MasterClass, LinkedIn Learning or Khan Academy, can be useful. Unless you're paying for it, though, it is often difficult to sort through the morass of free gibberish. If the class is free, that doesn't mean it's necessarily bad quality. It's just about finding the best sources for your needs. The key is to be laser-focused on what you want. You must take personal responsibility for what you need to learn, rather than rely on the Learning for Development team to decide.

> **KEY INSIGHT**
>
> You are the best placed person to understand what you need to learn for your job compared with what you already know.

Over the years, I have accumulated a list of reliable sources for the specific topics that are important to me. This takes work upfront. Fortunately, there are sites that can help you to mine sources and to aggregate the reading. For curated topics, I use three applications that differ according to the device:

- a premium version of Feedly (via desktop browser and mobile);
- Flipboard (on iPad and mobile);
- Twitter (via a premium version of Hootsuite, which I use mostly on the desktop).

In each case, I create specific topics or boards and handpick the sources I want to keep. Finally, when looking for a specific ad hoc question such as 'What is blockchain?' or 'How does 3D printing work?' I am inclined to start on YouTube rather than on Google.com. Whichever set of feeds you use, it's absolutely vital to revisit and update your lists and sources regularly. If need be, mark it in your calendar as a reminder to do so once at least every other month.

One more piece of advice for your ongoing learning ecosystem: don't hesitate to add your personal hobbies and passions into the mix of topics and sources. For example, I have boards on Flipboard on sleep, the Grateful Dead and my favourite NHL hockey team, the Philadelphia Flyers. To the extent you need extra impetus to help you navigate something new, an earnest interest in your passion will help draw you to overcome unfamiliar apps. Moreover, the personal passions will ensure you come back to the application with a certain alacrity. Of course, as the saying goes, all play and no work makes Jack a mere toy. But all work and no play makes Jack a dull boy.

Podcasts

I'm a big fan of podcasts. To wit, I've been podcasting myself for over 10 years. Podcasts offer an altogether different way of consuming information because they're audio recordings that you can listen to without having to look at a screen. With well over a million English-language podcasts available these days, it's hard not to find your subject in an audio format as well. Unlike blogs, the discovery mechanisms for podcasts need improvement. Unfortunately, there's no real shortcut to get the content but to listen to the recording. The good news is that, thanks to the intimacy of the audio being in your ear, you will quickly be able to detect whether you find the conversation engaging and authentic. My preferred service for listening to podcasts is Overcast and, in it, I can organize the podcasts according to the themes I am most interested in. You'll want to see if the format is as an interview or monologue. In both cases, the host will be important. Who are the guests? Is the sound production good? Do you like the host's voice? How long are the episodes on average? How frequently and consistently do they publish episodes? After finding the subjects and hosts you like, make sure that the length suits your lifestyle. I tend to split my podcast listening into three camps according to my activity: 15 to 20 minutes (eg commute), 30 to 45 (eg workout) and long form of over an hour (eg for longer travel times and walks).

The green meeting

As I mentioned before, I colour-code certain appointments in my calendar. Every week, I seek to have five 'green meetings', so called because they represent people I don't know. Often, I'm asked, how can I meet someone I don't know? Good question.

The reality is that, for some of these meetups, they're just acquaintances whom I don't know well. For others, I may have met them cursorily at a conference. Or they may have reached out to me after a speech or via social media. At conferences and gatherings, as everyone, I come back with a handful of business cards and then according to the perceived fit, I like to sort through them to connect and prolong the acquaintance by setting up a green meeting.

To make each meeting more robust, I will often do a summary check online of the person's writings and social media presence. However, importantly, I don't come to the meeting with an agenda. I like to let the magic happen, meeting the person face to face and connecting the dots as they occur. Through the discovery of the person, what they are doing and are interested in, I inevitably learn. The green meeting is a concrete manifestation of my karmic approach to leadership.

Sharing is caring

If learning should be a necessary and healthy component of your day, it's also important to share what you're learning. I encourage you to regularly and openly distribute what you find interesting with your network. Especially if your company uses an internal communication system such as Slack or Chatter (from Salesforce), I recommend regularly posting valuable reads, links or thoughts that are generally available to the entire workforce. The kicker is when you also qualify why you found the article of note. In this manner, you are showing what you are reading and learning, all the while demonstrating how you believe that sharing information is the way for you all to be stronger together.

By sharing what you're learning, you are doing three things:

- You are undoing the paradigm that knowledge is power. It's not.

- You are showing where you're at in terms of knowledge. In other words, you're implicitly showing where you are on the learning curve.
- You're setting the example for others to share.

By adding your personal insights, you'll also let your personality shine through. You can do the same on external-facing networks such as LinkedIn and Twitter, albeit with adjusted content. Whether it's the useful source you've unearthed or an insightful article you've read, you should be graciously sharing it out. To use a biological analogy, you want to be the heartbeat of the organization, circulating fresh and relevant knowledge through the body of your company.

Learning from mistakes

Among the most powerful ways to learn is through failure. However, it's equally true that talking about your failures or mistakes can be perceived as weakness or, in a corporate world, a career-limiting move. Especially in a culture where cut-throat colleagues will endeavour to take advantage of slip-ups, it's difficult to find the right balance. Depending on where you sit in the hierarchy, you'll need to know how to manage up. As far as leading your team is concerned, admitting to your mistakes, diving into the learnings you've made and sharing your feelings is a cogent way of inspiring others. There's a certain courage and vulnerability associated with owning up to your mistakes. Not only do we instinctively wish to avoid fessing up and lay the blame elsewhere, we inevitably don't take the time to ponder and share our learnings. At an organizational level, companies are quick to set up experiments, less quick to shut them down when they fail, and virtually never take the time to convert the

Your desire to try things out, make mistakes and make a fool of yourself is a big part of why being imperfect will be core to your long-term success.

learnings. Any agile method must include explicit time to digest and analyse failures. It's the definition of an experiment not to know the outcome in advance. Your desire to try things out, make mistakes and, at times, make a fool of yourself is a big part of why being imperfect will be core to your long-term success. That's the secret sauce of a true learning organization.

Making (brave) decisions

If these last two chapters have looked at how better to use your key resources, there's one last area that I'd like to touch on: When YOU LEAD, how do you make decisions, especially brave ones? With ownership, agency and conviction is the short answer. I have three principles when it comes to taking powerful decisions:

1 To what extent is the decision about fulfilling the brand's purpose?
2 How many *diverse* inputs have been used in the creation of the solution?
3 To what extent is the decision in line with the company's strategy?

Not that I wanted to shirk responsibility for a decision, but as I learned running Redken, when the team had gone through these elements (either implicitly or explicitly) and participated in the decision-making, the notion of commitment and likelihood of success were vastly improved.

Recap of key messages and actionable points

- Whatever your passion, don't hesitate to let the cat out of the bag. People would rather do business over time with someone with passion rather than a soulless person. Express yourself.

- You need to get ahead of the curve and put forward the best version of you, otherwise others will write their version of you for you.
- When you do something that fits your North Star setting, you know *why* you are doing it, and this will give you back extra energy over and above the amount you expended doing it.
- When telling stories, make sure to add the personal touch, for example by expressing your genuine emotion or saying how the story personally impacted you.
- On social media, allow yourself to follow your personal passions alongside your professional needs.
- You are the best placed person to understand what you need to learn compared with what you already know.
- You're never stronger than when you have a solid network that has your back, helps to stimulate you and provides you with relevant sources, insights and scoops.
- Your ability and desire to try things out, make mistakes and, at times, make a fool of yourself are a big part of why being imperfect will be core to your long-term success.

Endnotes

1. www.wsj.com/video/satya-nadella-the-learn-it-all-does-better-than-the-know-it-all/D8BC205C-D7F5-423E-8A41-0E921E86597C.html (archived at https://perma.cc/FDE4-HQBM)
2. Dial, M and Caleb Storkey (2017) *Futureproof: How to get your business ready for the next disruption*, Pearson FT Publishing International

CHAPTER NINE

Connecting the dots

CHAPTER OVERVIEW

To bring about transformation and raise engagement, you'll need to have the courage to be yourself and lead by example. If you show vulnerability and can accept your imperfections, others will feel permission to do the same. The best leader enables new leaders to emerge and flourish. As leader, you must help connect the dots and ideas, build the relationships and ensure that the work is meaningful. Being your authentic self will make you a better leader.

To the extent you've got to where you have by dint of hard work, intelligence and perhaps even some good fortune, this book is not about throwing out the baby with the bath water. In the end of the day, we are all striving as best we can. We've made decisions to the best of our abilities until now. What I am wishing to do with this book is bring a new slant to the way you operate going forward. It's not a revolution, but it will require some deep reflection. I exhort you to look at the patterns in your own life with candour. Connecting those dots will help you to understand yourself and identify your weak spots. For example, look for moments when you are likely to be triggered or things you have done repeatedly well or poorly.

Being better at leading, being more trustworthy, empathic and inspirational is a battle that is played out in the micro-moments far more than during the big, solemn decisions you must make. I liken it to going to a theatre with your spouse or partner. You watch the play together. You are side by side at the big event. But the complicity happens before in the selection of the play, in the planning to go and the journey there. Then, during the performance, in certain moments, you may do something small that says so much, such as look over or squeeze their hand. Afterwards, you discuss the play and share your emotions. This is the way you truly connect at work as well. You interact on a daily basis and in those smaller exchanges, you build rapport. A great test of a leader's authenticity is how they act when, by accident, meeting a colleague outside of work. It used to be that such moments were awkward and to be avoided. However, these encounters can provide a litmus test for your perceived integrity and sense of authenticity. It reflects the spirit of John Paul DeJoria, co-founder and current chair of Paul Mitchell Systems, who has often said that it's about how well you do what you do when no one is looking.

Strategic transformation: changing minds and culture

If you have read this far, you're hopefully aware that, at heart, this book is about encouraging meaningful transformation in the way you lead. It needs heightened self-awareness, an acceptance of self and a belief in the process. If digital is a great excuse to make wholesale change at your company, it's much less about the *digital* tech, and more about how to act differently in a digital *and* analogue existence. Fundamentally, it's about a change of mindset and, through a new way of behaving, of the company's culture. As you go about leading the change, you'll want to create a guiding North Star, translated into a strategy with purpose. What is the bigger purpose that is going to tap into a collective discretionary energy? What is the cornerstone strategy that will help you to refine the allocation of your limited resources? Your role as leader is to tell this story over and over again, making sure that everyone knows what their contribution is and to model the behaviour you want to see throughout the organization. The real transformation of culture happens through actions. You can't inspire change behind a closed door or wait until you can wordsmith the right missive. You've got to be prepared to show your genuine self through everyday actions and spontaneity.

As you go about leading the change, you'll want to create a guiding North Star, translated into a strategy with purpose.

Believe in the process: let go of some old tenets

Contrary to the belief that the end justifies the means, the best way forward is when the right means lead to a result. The *how* matters. The means are to lead to the desired outcome. It's perhaps subtle, but the order makes all the difference. The journey must be the focal point because as soon as one result is achieved, you're on to the next objective. The common denominator is the lasting culture you are installing with the codified language, behaviours and rites. In order to succeed, you need to believe in the process. Whenever you bring the horse (results) in front of the cart (process), you may reach your short-term objectives, but you'll surely lose out on long-term success. Just like with karma or philanthropy, as soon as the intention is twisted towards money-making aims, it inevitably loses its lustre. It may be a leap of faith, but you need to believe deep down that you're in business to do more than make money. Many individuals will nod their head in agreement with this, but when crunch time occurs, the old kneejerk principles quickly return. Old timers will feel the need to control what's going on. They will worry about people not doing what they ought to and want to micro-manage the situation. They will see shortcuts that will drive profitable gains, but that are too often at the expense either of the customer or of the long-term picture. **The most powerful transformation happens when you believe in the process and are willing for the results to be determined by the participants.** When you lead from within and listen earnestly, you'll unleash a durable form of energy. This doesn't obviate the need to craft numerical objectives and financial budgets to help navigate your path and bring fiduciary responsibility to your endeavours. Depending on the governance model, you'll have more or less latitude to drive the process. Being publicly traded or beholden to a shark-toothed vulture capitalist will limit your options. But unbridled and idealistic planning – such as seen in the excessive build-out of WeWork – is entirely undesirable. You need to create an equation that allows for sustainable growth. The objective is to create a responsible culture that is designed to be profitable. That's one reason why the Redken mission was so patently powerful: Earn a Better Living, Live a Better Life. It combined a meaningful purpose with profit. And the fact of the matter is that the latter mission really drove the former result.

Much like trying to steer creativity and impose love, you need to believe in the power of the process. You need to create an environment where both can flourish. Part of the magic comes when unanticipated connections lead to unexpected consequences.

The Connector-in-Chief: at your service

When YOU LEAD, you are the Connector-in-Chief and you're keen to join together pixels, people and purpose. As someone who listens openly and with intensity, you are able to relate disparate dots. When you lead from within, the connections become easier to spot. The distance between the dots is smaller for those who pay attention to them. If you're open to – even seeking – the serendipitous encounter, there's a bigger chance it will happen. By being aware of the different signals and willing to try new experiences, things naturally start to feel more connected.

Connecting pixels and curating content

In a world of plethoric information, value, influence and power are no longer generated by the knowledge you hold. Operating as an independent consultant, I have learned that the best way to go forward is to share my knowledge (eg through blog posts, articles and books). In so doing, I present my wares and exhibit my mindset, which is essentially why and how I get hired. It's also a fine way to earn trust. The key today is to be a conduit of curated information, to act as a trusted hub that knows how to pass along engaging content – to the necessary parties – in a timely manner.

Connecting people

As a leader, one of our key roles is to help build bridges between members of the team. Whether it's platoon commander, the quarterback of an American football team or the conductor of an orchestra, the leader knows how and why the team will work well together. The best Connector-in-Chief is able to see the lines and build the connections between people with diverse backgrounds and opinions, helping to tie them behind a unified mission. **Always think about who could be presented to whom,** facilitate relationships and make introductions that take into consideration the WIIFM (what's in it for me) for both parties.

Connecting to purpose

One of the most essential roles is to connect your team to the company's bigger purpose. You want to make everyone feel like they are genuinely contributing to the company's strategic ambitions. Alan Mulally, the ex-CEO of Ford, said that for a great leader, everything turns around the others, as opposed to oneself. In that same vein, your job is to make the others believe that they are working with and *for* the others. Within the context of an enterprise, you must seek to elevate your company's purpose, where it is seeking to contribute to stakeholders far greater and broader than merely the shareholder. **Your pivotal role is to keep making the connection between the daily grind and that higher purpose.** That's how one makes the purpose come alive. It's also how you will continue to tap into a stronger discretionary energy.

Building your network: it takes work

A dear friend of mine once observed how frequently she and I both tended to bump into old friends and acquaintances in wildly distant places. As the Disney song goes, 'It's a small world, after all'. The serendipity. The hazards of life. The sliding door of our encounters. But, for me, it's really just the consequence of having built up a strong and international network. Everything and everyone seem connected when you look for the signs. But you can't *expect* to run into an old friend (it's like karma) and you need to allow time for the unplanned encounter when it does come around. If you're always rushing against time, seeking order, efficiency and organization, and you don't allow for or have space for some chaos, you'll deprive yourself of some important connections. When I walk through a crowded place,

I like to register when I *don't* see someone I know, as if the world might all of a sudden be larger than expected. I feel like I owe it to the universe as a way to counterbalance the number of times I do randomly come across someone I know in far-off places. The fortuitous encounters, meanwhile, are more a consequence of a concerted effort to build a strong net*work*. There's work in the net. As I like to say, luck (or good fortune) comes before work only in the dictionary. (And that's true in many other languages including French, Dutch, Italian, Japanese, Portuguese, Russian, Spanish and Zulu.)

You're never stronger than when you have a solid network that has your back, helps to stimulate you and provides you with relevant sources, insights and scoops. Your network thus becomes a significant resource. Echoing the motto that Nadella embodies at Microsoft, when YOU LEAD, you adopt a position of humility and are prepared to ask questions for help and explanation rather than insist on total prescience. If you systematically ask questions, your team will learn to come to you with answers and solutions.

> *You're never stronger than when you have a solid network that has your back.*

KEY INSIGHT

It's better to consider yourself at the service of those around you rather than be a pontificator of lessons learned.

Imperfection: embrace your foibles

No one likes to hear they're below average or imperfect, yet we all are to some degree. It may be that we are shorter in physical height, less good at the *New York Times* crossword puzzle or below average at throwing darts. It's not such a big deal. As successful leaders, meanwhile, chances are we are over-achievers and have grown up to have a higher opinion of ourselves than might objectively be the case. But we can't be above average at *all* things. How self-aware are you? Would others close to you agree with your self-evaluation?

The trick is to rein in our sense of confidence and recognize when and where we might be less good. Not only will such an avowal help to draw up a more complementary and effective team around you, it will make you more believable and appreciable. While I encourage sufficient vulnerability to be aware and admit your weaknesses, I also insist on wishing to be better as an individual. Admitting an imperfection does not absolve you from trying to improve. For example, it's not because I feel and believe that I have a short fuse that I should allow myself to be blow frequently. You need to have the courage and drive to improve your standards and to elevate the debate. I've seen many an older executive believe they're allowed to be curmudgeonly or curt because 'they've earned the right'. Others might lament, 'I'm too old to change'. Nonsense. One should always seek to improve and take the higher road. This is not just our civic duty. It's a question of sense of self and dignity. I'd even suggest it's the healthier route. I cite the case when choosing a surgeon for an important operation. One typically will want to have the best surgeon possible, right? But, if that brilliant surgeon has terrible manners and treats the attending physician, nurses, orderlies and all-important anaesthesiologist with disdain, there can be ramifications on the outcome. Moreover, the surgeon's ability to listen during the initial phases of discovery and diagnosis may be impeded by an over-sized ego. And, when they come to visit you post-op, what kind of bedside manner can you expect? Of course, you want the best operation, but the final outcome will also depend on the team around the surgeon. How connected is the surgeon to the original mission that attracted them to the profession? Or are you, the patient, just another number to notch up en route to a summit? Even the best surgeon needs to lead appropriately on and off the operating table. No one can be perfect, especially under stress. But that's when and where you discover the true leaders.

Seek your North, not perfection

When you're lining up your North Star, I'd much rather a directionally correct setting rather than a precise and rigidly perfect due North. It's my conviction that **a team bonded by a common and uplifting purpose will be far more powerful and committed to overcome the challenges, countenance the tough conversations and deliver the results.**

KEY INSIGHTS

Embrace your foibles. Recognize your weaknesses. Look for complementary partners. Always strive for better. Be wary of seeking perfection.

Fair and firm: understand and be understood

I learned from Pat Parenty the value of being at once fair and firm. I liken these two qualities to being intelligent. I describe intelligence as making sense. It is the product of understanding (making sense of what you hear) and being understood (giving sense through your expression). This echoes what Stephen Covey wrote for the fifth habit in *The 7 Habits of Highly Effective People:* your task is first to listen and understand.[1] It involves two important preconditions. First, in order to listen and understand optimally, you must dissolve the ego and remove your preconceptions. By making the effort to understand deeply, you have a far greater chance to be fair and just in your resolve. The second action is to be firm in your judgement and the way you express yourself. Underwriting your firmness is the ability to be clear in your expression. To be firm is to make sure that you are well understood. You need to lean in whenever you see that your message isn't getting through.

Another important point is that it is fair AND firm, not fair *but* firm. These two values do not live in opposition or as a qualifier of the other. You must seek to be fair and firm in equal doses.

Business as a force for good: inside and out

One of my underlying beliefs is that business not only can be but *must be* a force for good. Not that unethical people and malevolent companies won't succeed. They can and do. But, without tapping into a higher cause, they are leaving a lot on the table. Such poverty of humanity will be unhealthy over the long term and, moreover, the risks of being exposed have risen dramatically over the last couple of decades. Even privately held, tight-knit companies are having their dirty laundry aired. The news headlines continue to be populated with major scandals, some of which have had penal consequences for their top management, including in recent years at Volkswagen, Orange, Renault-Nissan, Liberty Tax, Waffle House and Landcastle Title. But the law is not and cannot be the final determinant. With so many new technologies, usages and opportunities unfolding daily, the legislators will likely continue to be latecomers to the party. As leaders, we need to establish our own internal law or code of ethics. As such, it will be up to the individuals at the helm to set the course and boundaries that delineate, for each company, the ethical framework to which they will hold *themselves* accountable. You'll want to describe sample behaviours for greater clarity. In other words, you should describe what acceptable and unacceptable actions look like.

As my friend Giles Gibbons, CEO and co-founder of Good Business, says, doing good is also good for business. To have a strong North Star is to have a moral compass, something that can't be delegated to the legal team. The laws are just not able to keep par with the evolving technologies. All manner of organizations, from commercial airplane to soap manufacturers, from the military to the local council, from NGOs to charities, are digitalizing, using increasing amounts of technological tools, devices and platforms. This will involve, among other significant areas, communications, data management and automation. With managers and programmers down deep in the ranks, there are many actions that are hard to keep tabs on from above; for example, in the encoding of artificial intelligence, setting up of programmatic marketing, data collection practices or the installation of behind-the-screen cookies. A lack of understanding of and transparency in how these systems, lying deep within the enterprise, work will do nothing to improve a company's trustworthiness. You may soon find your own employees with a sense of ethics applying pressure on you for better business practices, as they will not be keen to be associated with unethical methods.

To the extent we are spending a large chunk of our waking hours at work, it really makes sense that we spend our time in ways that are aligned with our personal values and North Star setting. Not only are consumers also citizens, we have employees who are family members and participants in local communities. When we leave the office and feel good about ourselves and the work we've accomplished, we will have a positive energy that will spread and shine without the office walls. If we do right by our moral compass, we won't feel like we need to avoid conversations or duck our eyes at the 'tricky' questions. As strong leaders, we need to seek to create an environment that is better for the employees, customers, stakeholders and, ultimately, for the bottom line. **Doing things that matter is a way to create an infinite well of extra energy.** Thus, it's even good for you, too.

If we say that the best measure of performance is the share price, it's a challenge to directly correlate and equally impossible to refute the relationship of quality of a product or service with shareholder value. You'll need to have a performing product, but it doesn't suffice. As I've pointed out previously in this book, there are studies that correlate higher empathy, meaningfulness and purpose with superior performances versus companies that lack these qualities. It may be a messier route, but it becomes far more rewarding – including for the bottom line – when YOU LEAD by being yourself. It's a healthier path and it will make you a better leader. The best route is not to have two different selves – one at work and one at home – but to focus on *one* self.

One final question: How do you measure what is important about your work for others around you?

Endnote

1.   Covey, S (1989) *The 7 Habits of Highly Effective People*, 1st edn, Free Press

Index

NB: page numbers in *italic* indicate figures or tables

5G   6
7 Habits of Highly Effective People, The   220
9/11 terrorist attacks, New York   1–2, 72, 73, 172
10 Minute Mind, The   178
'24-hour rule'   192

Adidas   12
affective empathy   103
Airbnb   9, 183
Alibaba   29
Alphabet   34, 40
Amazon   9, 29
   Alexa   9
   Amazon Leadership Principles   41
   as a benchmark   163
   governance   40–41
   physical stores   183
   Zappos   157
'AND Rule', the   55
Android   96
AOL   24
Apple   29
   corporate brand   34
   iPhone   9, 34, 96
   Jobs, Steve   89–90
   'painting the back side of the fence'   138
   share prices   36, 37
   vision statement   15, 62, 149
Aramco   39
Aristotle   12
Armstrong, David Malet   161
Art of Gathering, The   63
artificial intelligence (AI)   6, 46, 167
Audible   9
authenticity   17, 18
   and likeability   99
   vulnerability, showing   75, 89

Baidu   29
Baran, Chris   45
BAT   29
Beats   34
Beaussier, Alexandre   161
Ben & Jerry's   136–37, 141
Bettencourt, Liliane   38
Bezos, Jeff   15, 40, 149, 164
Bitcoin   9
Black Lives Matter movement   12, 136
Board of Governors (BoG) principle   185, 193
Bonobos   9
Borders   24
Boyé, Clément   58, 74
Brand Tattoo test   38, 134–35, *135*
Branson, Richard   125, 126
   'W is for Weakness'   125
bravado   106
Brillat-Savarin, Jean Anthelme   179
Brin, Sergey   40
Burger King   150
Burgess, C and Burgess, M   10
Business Roundtable   33, 46, 124
Businessolver   104, 105
Byung-chul, Lee   36

calendar, colour-coding your   186
Canon   149–50
causes, supporting   137
Chanel   34, 41
change management   25
   and messiness   79
chaos theory   79
CHECK mindset   93–94
   and community   132
   courage   106–10
      vs bravado   106
      'colours', your   107–08
      and humility   110

curiosity 95–97
  green meetings 97
  qualities, important 95–96
empathy 102–05
  affective empathy 103
  and business results 104
  cognitive empathy 103
  'empathy gap' 104
humility 97–102
  and courage 110
  and ego 98
  forcing 98
  purposes of 99–100
  and trust 100–02
  and weakness 102
karmic 110–15
  expectations, letting go of 111
  'karmic capitalism' 114
chief digital officer 24
chief ethics officer 48
chief storyteller 82
Chiu, C-Y *et al* 101
Chobani 142
ChooseMyCompany 119
Chouinard, Yvon 43, 47
Chrome 96
Clarins 34
Clayton, Steve 82
cognitive empathy 103
Cohen, Ben and Greenfield, Jerry 136
Collins, Jim 3, 110
Colonna, Jerry 74
'colours', your 107–08
Compaq 150
concentric extensions 31
conflict management 192–93
  '24-hour rule' 192
  Board of Governors (BoG)
    principle 193
conglomerate diversification 31
congruency 73
  in communications *141*, 141–42
Conley, Chip 114
content management 149
conversation, role of 180–81
Cordant Group 45
cortisol 131
courage 106–10

vs bravado 106
'colours', your 107–08
and humility 110
Coursera 205
Covey, Stephen 110, 220
Covid-19 pandemic 3, 7, 113
  remote working during 60–61
curiosity 95–97
  green meetings 97
  qualities, important 95–96
Curry, Latia 13, 14
Customer Experience (CX) 127, 149
  measuring 156
  perceptions vs reality 150
customer lifetime value 168

Dacor 36
Daimler 34
Dalle, François 65, 73
'data fluency' 50
data management 222
  analogue and digital,
    combining 156, 158
  data and empathy 160
  data democratization 156, 158,
    167
  data governance 49–50
    breaches 50
  ontology, role of 160–61
  training, employee 162
decision-making 210
DeJoria, John Paul 213
delegation 187
Deloitte 16
Descartes, René 78
Dial, Nathaniel 106–07
Dial, Victor 10
diet, role of 179
differentiation, and identity 66–67
'digital mountain', the 20, *21*, 25
'digital native' culture 149
digital transformation 19, 22, 25, 48
  AND mindset, cultivating a 55
DiSC personality types 188
Discourse on Method 78
discretionary energy 87, 214
Donaldson, Lufkin & Jenrette
  (DLJ) 28

Drucker, Peter   33
Duarte, Nancy   82
Dujardin, Ludovic   178
Dunne, Ronan   10, 107, 199

Easterbrook, Steve   159
Edward Scissorhands   67
Elegant Universe, The   79
email use   196–97
   response times   198
   tips for   202
emojis   203
emoticons   203
emotional intelligence   190
empathy   102–05
   affective empathy   103
   and business results   104
   cognitive empathy   103
   'empathic muscle', our   80
   'empathy gap'   104
Empathy Business, The   104
Employee Experience (EX)   127–28
Employees First   121
energy, managing   63, 222
essence, your   *see* 'North Star' setting,
      your
ethics
   chief ethics officer   48
   data governance   49–50
   ethical framework, creating a   48,
      166
   marketing promises   141
   profit, ethical   46–47
   value chains, ethical   47–48
Eurostar   153–54
exercise, role of   179
expectations, letting go of   111

Facebook   29, 40
FaceTime   197
'faire de la comm'   17
feedback
   accepting   76, 187
   giving   188–89
Feedly   9, 206
Firefox   96
Firms of Endearment   3
Flipboard   9, 206

Ford Motor Company   108, 115, 217
Ford, Henry   15
founding family, importance of
     38–39, 42–43, 44
   transitioning from   44–45
free will   68
Futureproof   201

GAFAM   29
Gaiman, Neil   82
Garcia, Jerry   92, 93, 94, 100, 120
geographic growth   31
Gibbons, Giles   221
GIFs   203
Gilt   163
Glassdoor   119
Global Entrepreneurship Monitor
     (GEM)   97
Glossier   88, 163
Goldberg, Bruce   114
Good Business   221
Good to Great   3, 110
Google   17, 29, 206
   Alphabet   34
   governance   40
   outdoor advertising   183
Goz, Aviad   58
Grateful Dead, The   92–94, 120, 132,
     206
green meetings   97, 207–08
Greene, Brian   79
'guilt culture'   129
Guinness   133
Guttman, Howard   73

Handley, Ann   114
Harley-Davidson   46–47, 133, 141
   Harley-Davidson Owners Group
     (HOGS)   135–36
Harman   36
Harvard Business Review (HBR)
     104
Havas Meaningful Brands® study
     2019   62, 87
head office culture   33
Headspace   178
Heartificial Empathy   80, 103, 160,
     201

HIPPO (highest paid person's opinion)
   63, 164
Holmes, Elizabeth   45
Hootsuite   206
horizontal extensions   31
Howard, Lucy   125
hugs, benefits of   130–31
human resources, importance of   25
humility   97–102
   and courage   110
   and ego   98
   forcing   98
   purposes of   99–100
   and trust   100–02
   and weakness   102
hybrid companies   34, 36, 39

iCloud   34
inbox, clearing your   7–8
infrastructure-oriented companies   151
Inside-Out model   *121*, 121–22, 131
   at Redken   121–22, *122*
Insights   188
Instagram   199
Institut Français d'Opinion Publique
   (IFOP)   61, 126
International Data Corporation (IDC)
   97
Isaacson, Walter   138
iTunes   34
IwheelShare   88

Jobs, Steve   90, 138
Jope, Alan   107
Journal of Management   101
Jung, Carl   54

Kaepernick, Colin   11–12
Kalanick, Travis   45
karma   110–15
   expectations, letting go of   111
   'karmic capitalism'   114
Kent Meehan, Paula   45, 72, 128
Kering   34
Khan Academy   205
Kindle   9
Kodak   24, 150
Kristiansen, Kjeld Kirk   64–65

Lancôme   38
Landcastle Title   221
Lao Tsu   95
Last Ring Home, The   106
Leadership Survey 2020   105
learning
   green meetings   97, 207–08
   mistakes, learning from   209–10
   online   205–07
   podcasts   207
   sharing your   208–09, 216
LEGO   64–65
Lesh, Phil   92, 93
Liberty Tax   221
likeability   99
like-for-like growth   31
LinkedIn   96, 203, 209
   LinkedIn Learning   205
   Marketing Solutions Blog   16
   profile, your   199
logistics-oriented companies   151
L'Oréal   28, 45, 71, 73, 171, 172,
   196
   arrogance, perceived   98–99, 100
   food, importance of   179
   founding family involvement
      38–39
   as a hybrid company   34, 36, 38
   paradox of management   65
   R&D laboratories   159
   slogan   149
   see also Redken
loyalty, earning   127–28
LVMH   34
Lyft   8

Mahoney, Peter   129
marketing-oriented companies   151
MarketingProfs   114
marketing promises   141
Marks & Spencer   150, 151
Mars   41
MasterClass   205
McDonald's   159
McRaven, William   178
meditation, role of   110, 178
Meehan, John   128
meetings, productive   184

Board of Governors (BoG)
    principle 185, 193
chairman, role of 185–86
face-to-face 183
meeting-itis 183
merchandise, branded 134
mergers and acquisitions (M&A)
    32
failure rate 33
Microsoft 29, 50, 82, 218
Mincey, Ann 129, 130
mindfulness 177–78
Miron-Spektor, Ella 65
mistakes, accepting 161
Monarch Airlines 149
Monzo 9
moral compass, your 30, 222
Mulally, Alan 115, 217
music, role of 181–82
Myers-Briggs Type Indicator (MBTI)
    188

Nadella, Satya 196, 218
NASA 133
Nayar, Vineet 121
Net Promoter Score (NPS) 155
Neumann, Adam 40
NEWS Coaching 58
Nike 11–12
'North Star' setting, your 4, 56–60,
    58, 222
    benefits of a strong 62
    checking in with 178–79
    core values, your 59
    crafting your 58
    perfection, aiming for 220
    'personal brand', your 200–01
    personal vs professional 59–60
    success, defining 57

Omnisend 50
ontology 160–61
open rates, of CRM emails 165, 167
open-door policies 193–94
OpenPartners 9
opportunism (growth model) 32
Orange 221
Overcast 207

ownership structure *31*
oxytocin 131

PACTE Act no. 2019–486 61
Page, Larry 40
Parenty, Pat 72, 73, 101, 128, 220
Parker, Priya 63
Parmar, Belinda 104
Partner Mindset 123–24, *124*
Patagonia 43, 46, 47, 141
Paul Mitchell Systems 213
Pawshake 9
PayPal 9
Peak 114
Pepsi 90
perfection 141, 218–20
'personal brand', your 198–200
Petco 123
Petit BamBou 178
Peugeot 42
Physiology of Taste, The 179
podcasts 207
political stance, taking a 12–14
    steps to 13–14
Politics 12
Power of Positive Thinking (PPT)
    132
privately-held firms 39, 41–42
Procter & Gamble (P&G) 34
product-oriented companies 151,
    159
profitability-oriented companies 151
profit, ethical 46–47
programmatic marketing 222
promotions, internal focus on
    151–52
propaganda 17
publicly-traded companies 39–41
Puddicombe, Andy 178
Purpose-Driven Life, The 102

quantum tunnelling 79

RALLY 13
RatedPeople 9
Reboot 74
Redken 132, 172, 185, 210
    brand loyalty 127, 128

conflict resolution   192–93
congruency   73
distributor network   101
haircare packaging   138
Inside-Out model   *122*
   Redken Performing Artists
     (RPAs)   69–70, 121–22
   Redken Tribe   69–70, 122, 131
   Redkenites   121
   Kent Meehan, Paula   45, 72, 128
   literature for education   138
   merchandise   133–34
   mission   215
   Power of Positive Thinking (PPT)
     132
   purpose   72–73
   Redken Hug   129–30, 138
   Symposium   133
   wages   128
remote working   7, 60–61
remuneration   191–92
   and purpose   129, 191
Renault-Nissan   221
Rhodes, Monique   178
Richardson, Louis   82
Rosekind, Mark   180
Ryan, Kevin   163

Safari   96
Salesforce   208
sales-oriented companies   151
Salon Resource Group   129
Samsung   34, 36, 150
   Cheil   36
   Samsung Electronics   36, 37
   Shilla   36
Satir, Virginia   131
Schmidt, Eric   40
School of Unlearning, The   22
Schueller, Eugene   38
Sculley, John   90
Seligman, Martin   98
'servant leadership'   101
Shazam   34
Siri   9
Sisodia, R and Sheth, J   3
Slack   202, 208
sleep, role of   180

smartphones   6, 198
   in meetings   185–86
   notifications, managing   203–04
social media, using   9, 203
   accountability   17
   in B2B   16
   community, building a   132
   Dunne, Ronan   10, 107, 199
   groups, creating   203
   response times   198
   'social employee'   10–11, 14
Sorrell, Martin   202
Sovignet, Audrey   88
spam   18
Stanton, Andrew   82
Starling Bank   9
State of Workplace Empathy   104,
   105
Storkey, Caleb   201
storytelling, art of   81–82, 201
STOXX 600 Index   62
sunk costs   24
Swinscoe, Adrian   155
Syniti   82

Tencent   29
text messaging   202–03
'thank you', saying   18–90
Theranos   45
Thiel, Peter   106
Thomson, William (Lord Kelvin)   78
Thurow, Lester   197
Ticketmaster   94
Ticketron   94
time management   63–64, 182
   calendar, colour-coding your   186
   expecting the unexpected   183–84
   meetings, productive   184
     Board of Governors (BoG)
       principle   185, 193
     chairman, role of   185–86
     face-to-face   183
     meeting-itis   183
     open-door policies   193–94
T-Mobile   50
toll free contact numbers   157
Tor   96
touchpoints, customer   156

Transcendent Function 54
tribe, belonging to a 67, 69, 70
truth, power of 81
TUI 149
Twitter 17, 96, 203, 206, 209
    Dunne, Ronan 10
    notifications, managing 204

Uber 8, 45, 47–48
Uldrich, Jack 22
Ullmann, Phillip 45, 129
Ulukaya, Hamdi 142
Unilever 34, 107, 136
uniqueness, crafting 138, 140
'unlearning' 23, 80, 96

value chains, ethical 47–48
vanity metrics 164
Verizon Consumer Group 10, 107,
    199
Virgin 124–25, 126, 142
Volkswagen 221
voting rights 39–41
vulnerability, showing 75, 89

Waffle House 221
Walmart 9
Warren, Rick 102
We Company, The 40
Weiss, Emily 88
Wells Fargo 149
WestJet Airlines 110–13, 113–14
WeWork 40, 215
WhatsApp 197, 202
    notifications, managing 204
Whitehead, Alfred 161
wifi on trains 154
WIIFM (what's in it for me) 217
Wikileaks 48
'W is for Weakness' 125
WPP 202

Yahoo! 24, 150
YouTube 110, 111, 205, 206

Zappos 157
Zehnder, Egon 99, 110
Zero to One 106
Zoom 60
Zuckerberg, Mark 40